The Story of a 'Remarkable British Archaeologist'

Published by:
The Northamptonshire Archaeological Society

© Copyright 2010
Dennis Jackson and Northamptonshire Archaeological Society

This book is available from:
The Northamptonshire Archaeological Society
See our website for further details
www.northants-archaeology.org.uk

Front cover: Dennis on a watching brief on the route of the M40 in south Northamptonshire
Back cover: Reconstruction of the Wootton Hill Farm Iron Age enclosure by Alex Thompson

ISBN 978-0-9507151-4-8

Printed and bound by:
Information Press
Southfield Road
Eynsham
Oxford OX29 4JB
www.informationpress.com

Contents

Preface

Professor Barry Cunliffe

When writing about the British Iron Age in the early 1970s I once bewailed the lack of evidence from the East Midlands, but was quickly taken to task by a friend from Northampton who said "But you must meet Dennis Jackson – he is totally revolutionizing things here single handed" How right she was – by the end of the 1970s Dennis had excavated seventeen Iron Age settlements. More were to follow in the next two decades and the total now stands at more than forty! This was impressive enough but what was more important was that many of his excavations were of complete settlements – Twywell, Brigstock, Wakerley, Aldwincle, Grendon and Wootton Hill Farm – all of which have now taken their rightful place in the literature as classic-type sites.

But Dennis was doing more than just excavating sites – he was exploring whole landscapes as they came under threat from large-scale ironstone quarry or gravel working. Remains of all periods were explored with equal care from the famous Bronze Age barrow at Earls Barton to the fascinating Roman iron working furnaces at Laxton and the prolific Anglo-Saxon cemetery at Wakerley – each one making a major contribution to the knowledge of its period.

Dennis's active and highly creative life in archaeology is a remarkable story of forty years of devotion charting the determination of one man to rescue the fast-disappearing remains of our past undeterred by pressure from quarry managers, unhelpful bureaucracy and bitter winters. His story, told here with characteristic modesty, reflects, in microcosm, the coming of age of British archaeology. It began in the distant past, in the early 1960s when much of the work was in the hands of gifted amateurs, and takes us through the frenetic phase of rescue archaeology in the late 60s and 70s when most of what was achieved was done by skilled practitioners like Dennis who were prepared to devote themselves single-mindedly to the task. The story ends in the more anonymous world of units and contract archaeology dominated by competitive tendering and rigorous cost-cutting sampling. Nowadays things are moving on to a more enlightened vision, in which the success of a project is measured in terms of new knowledge and increased public understanding.

There is nothing in these emerging attitudes that would surprise Dennis. Throughout his professional life, as his story makes so abundantly clear, his prime aim has been to use archaeological data to write narratives, be it of a site, a landscape or a period of time. For him the satisfaction lies in publishing his results quickly and accessibly, so that they are available to all, and using them to contribute to the broader picture. It is no exaggeration to say that his chapter "Reflections on Iron Age Excavations in the County" could not have been written without his own massive contribution to the database: it is a significant contribution to British prehistory.

FACING PAGE
Dennis Jackson examining a piece of ironstone. Publicity photograph taken by the British Steel Corporation in 1971.

This book offers an insight into the dedication and achievements of a remarkable British archaeologist: it is also a significant contribution to the history of our vibrant discipline.

Barry Cunliffe Oxford, September 2009

Acknowledgements

An archaeological career is a team effort. From the family support that got me out of bed in the mornings; to the fellow workers who helped in all conditions and to those who made sense of it all through post-excavation work, I am deeply indebted. It would be remiss of me not to mention just a few names from this extensive cast list and the many others who helped along the way.

I spent a lot of time working in the ironstone quarries operated by British Steel in the Corby area, and without their unfailing support and co-operation much of our work would have been impossible. Managers and workers at all levels were usually, but not always, understanding and prepared to do whatever they could to help, even if it sometimes affected their own schedules. Arthur Blott, the manager of these quarries, deserves my particular thanks along with the many unnamed digger drivers and machine operators who worked for British Steel at this time.

A roll call of all those who helped on excavations is impossible and I hope I am excused in mentioning just those who made a contribution over a number of years. In the early days, it was difficult to find experienced helpers and I was fortunate to have the assistance of two students from Kettering Grammar School – Brian Dix and Terry Panter – who belonged to the Archaeological Society of the school run by their inspiring headmaster John Steane. Terry worked with me on a number of sites, but sadly died following a motor cycle accident. Brian provided valuable assistance during excavations and on post-excavation work for many years. Other people whose help was invaluable in the early years were Reg Eady, Jim Pollack, Jon Small and Dick Hollowell. I am also grateful to Alex Rollings, a school master and excellent photographer, who was always around when I needed him.

During the 1970s I had valuable assistance from Pat Foster and Peter Woods who both provided regular support on excavations and also spent many hours preparing illustrations and plans for published reports. Pat, in particular, provided constant encouragement and support whilst excavating the important sites at Wakerley, Weekley and Brigstock. Others who helped at this time include Burl Bellamy, Richard Harper, John Stapleton and Roy Turland. I was also grateful for the assistance of students from Northampton Grammar School including my son Stephen, Andy Beavan and Dave Baxter.

In later years, I had valuable support from Gill Johnston (and Pat Foster again) and my friend Alan Williams, who worked on the excavations we carried out as contractors and provided much needed support during difficult times in our relationship with the Northamptonshire Archaeology Unit.

At the other end of the cycle I am grateful to everyone who helped with the post-excavation work and the publication of reports. In addition to those already mentioned above – especially Brian Dix, Pat Foster and Peter Woods – this also includes Tim Ambrose, Roy Turland, David Neal and the staff of the Ancient

Monuments Drawing Office. I also need to thank the two principal editors of Northamptonshire Archaeology, Tony Brown and Martin Tingle who published the majority of my reports.

The number of fellow archaeologists who have provided inspiration is of course legion but I will mention only a few who I had the privilege to meet. Dr Dennis Harding played a key role in starting my career as a professional archaeologist by bringing my work to the attention of the Ministry of Works. Professor C.F.C. Hawkes helped with the report on the Earls Barton barrow and I found meeting him and Sir Mortimer Wheeler inspirational in my early days. Also in this category I would include Leo Biek, who was the Chief Scientist for the Ministry of Works in the 1960s and whose friendship and support was invaluable at a time when I was very new to the world of professional archaeology. In the 1970s my base for writing reports was the Institutue of Archaeology in Oxford and I am grateful to Professor Cunliffe for arranging this and for providing his Research Assistant Tim Ambrose to help write my major reports. Whilst working at the Institute, Roger Goodburn put my name forward for election as a Fellow of the Society of Antiquaries (FSA), and I appreciate his support. Finally, and at the local level, I cannot fail to mention the inspiration provided by Dick Hollowell, undoubtedly the father of Northamptonshire Archaeology.

I must also pay tribute to the support provided by the two main archaeological societies in the county; the Upper Nene Archaeological Society and the Northamptonshire Archaeological Society. I have been proud to be a member of both societies and have benefitted enormously from the advice and encouragement provided by other members over the years. The societies have made a major contribution towards improving people's understanding of the county's past by recording and publishing the results of archaeological activity in such a professional and accessible manner.

None of this would have been possible of course without the unfailing contribution of my late wife Betty, who provided a constant source of emotional and practical support throughout my career. This required considerable personal sacrifice and family commitment on her part to enable me to pursue such a career. But never complaining and always supportive, Betty was the perfect Assistant Director. She remains much missed but her promotion was long overdue.

Finally, I must thank all those who have helped bring this book to fruition. My son, Stephen, provided the initial inspiration and helped with much of the text, and his wife, Nancye Church, spent many hours re-drawing plans and laying out the text. I am also grateful to Pat Foster, John Small, Pat Chapman and Andy Chapman who read through various versions and made constructive comments throughout. My good friend and neighbour Joyce provided much needed support and encouragement throughout this process. Any errors or omissions are of course all mine.

Dennis Jackson, Northampton, August 2010

Introduction

"The land of shadows wilt thou trace
And look nor know each other's face,
The present mixed with reasons gone
And past and present all as one,
Say maiden can thy life be led
To join the living with the dead,
Then trace thy footsteps on with me
We're wed to one eternity"

John Clare, An Invite To Eternity

In the winter of 1899, my grandfather Thomas Jackson and his young family left their home in Washingley for the first and last time. The Jackson family had lived in this small village on the border of Huntingdonshire and Northamptonshire for five successive generations. Thomas 30, and his wife Emma, 28, along with their two-year-old son Thomas, were the first members of the family forced to leave their village home to seek work elsewhere. It would not have been an easy move.

After a period spent drifting between various villages in Huntingdonshire, the Jackson family finally settled in Southwick, just over the county border in Northamptonshire. This was only about 10 miles from Washingley but it was a highly significant move. It led to my father meeting a young girl in Southwick named Katie Hill, who would eventually become my mother, and it placed the Jackson family quite firmly on the Northamptonshire side of the county boundary where they stayed for the rest of the lives. By the time I was born, some thirty years later, the Jacksons were well established in this north-eastern part of Northamptonshire and I naturally inherited a love of their adopted county.

Although I eventually followed the natural drift westwards towards the county town of Northampton, the north-east part of the county has remained a constant source of inspiration throughout my life. The family ties that remained in this part of the county also meant that this is where my initial interest and involvement in archaeology was first developed and where I subsequently carried out much of my work.

I have been very fortunate in being able to do so much archaeological work in the county – both in the north-east and in other parts of the area. Hopefully, I have been able to make a small contribution to our understanding of the historic environment of Northamptonshire and the lives of people who lived here before us. By presenting this story of a 'Northamptonshire Archaeologist' I hope to repay readers for just a little of the enormous satisfaction and reward I have gained from my work in the county.

I have tried to provide an account of interest to both the general reader and the archaeological specialist. It is divided into three parts; the first two parts provide a broadly chronological account of my life and work. Part 1 starts with a brief outline of the Jackson family's life in their home parish of Washingley in Huntingdonshire, and in Chapter 2, I follow my grandparents move to Northamptonshire; my father's participation in the First World War and the subsequent marriage of my parents in Southwick. It is at this point that I enter the story, and in Chapter 3 I describe my childhood and early working life as a bricklayer up to the mid-1960s.

In Part 2, I discuss my career as a professional archaeologist, which I have divided into three chapters covering the 1960s, 1970s and 1980s respectively. In Chapter 4, I summarise the main excavations carried out in the 1960s, including a Saxon weaving shed at Upton; Neolithic and Bronze Age burials at Aldwincle; Iron Age settlements at Twywell and Aldwincle; a Roman bridge at Aldwincle; a Bronze Age burial at Earls Barton and an Anglo-Saxon cemetery at Wakerley. Chapter 5 continues the story into the 1970s and includes accounts of major excavations of Iron Age and Romano-British sites in the Welland valley – at Wakerley, Harringworth and Gretton – and at Weekley, just outside Kettering. In Chapter 6, I trace the effect of the changing nature of archaeological work from the 1980s onwards and include accounts of excavations carried out on Iron Age sites at Stanwell Spinney, Wellingborough and Wootton Hill Farm, together with a major Roman iron working site at Laxton.

Part 3 contains some personal reflections; in Chapter 7, I look back on the highs and lows of my archaeological career and some of the changes that have taken place in archaeology over this time; in Chapter 8, I attempt to summarise some of the lessons we have learned about the Iron Age in Northamptonshire from the excavations and other work that I have been involved in over the past 50 years. In Chapter 9, I put forward a personal theory on the function of pit alignments based on sites I have excavated in the county.

The appendices include a proposed chronology of Iron Age pottery and a summary of radiocarbon dates for the main Iron Age sites included in the text, kindly prepared by Andy Chapman. Further detailed information on where I have carried out work in the county and where and when the results have been published is also included in the appendices.

I hope that this account of my career will be of interest and benefit to anyone interested in the county's history and any archaeologists fortunate – or foolhardy – enough to follow in my footsteps in the future.

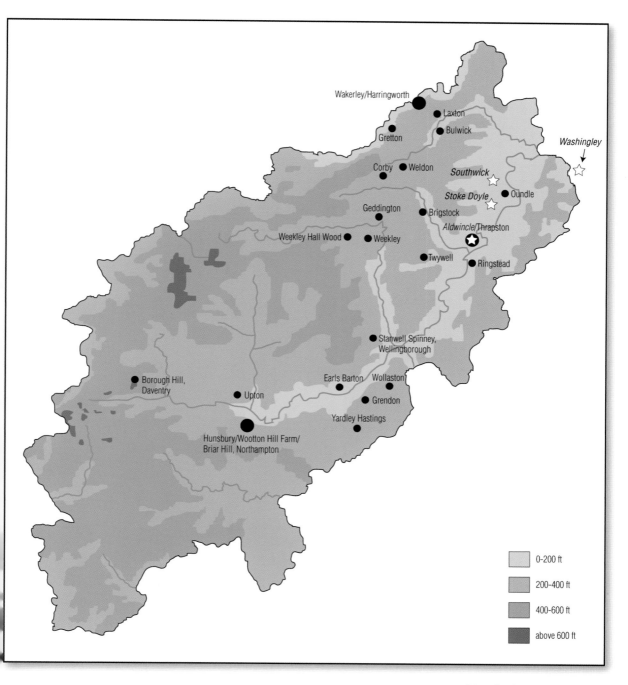

Map of main sites mentioned in the text.

PART ONE

Prehistory

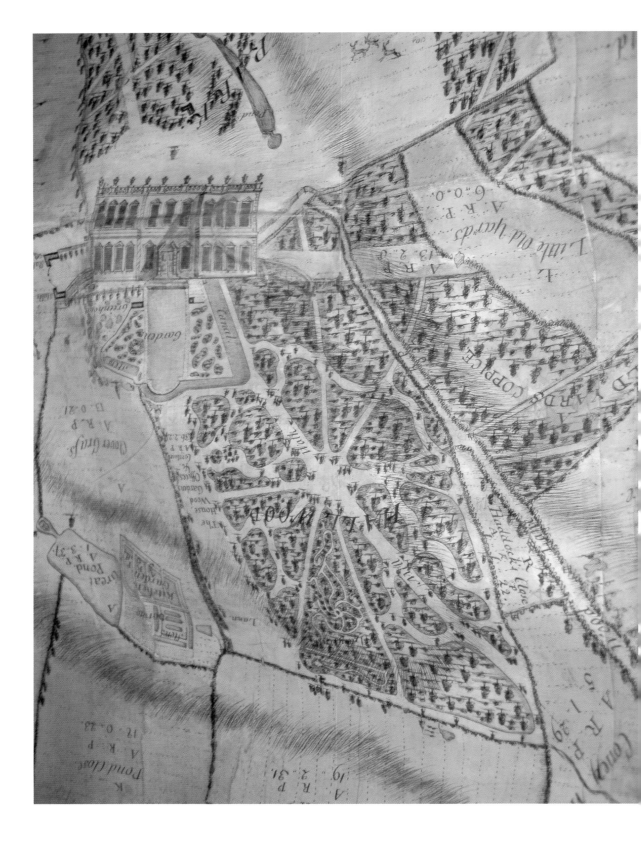

CHAPTER ONE

Washingley and the Jacksons

Toiling in the naked fields,
Where no bush a shelter yields,
Needy Labour dithering stands,
Beats and blows his numbing hands,
And upon the crumping snows
Stamps, in vain, to warm his toes.

John Clare, Address To Plenty

A Home Parish

The Jackson's home parish of Washingley, Huntingdonshire, lies eight miles south-east of Peterborough on a ridge of high land between the Nene Valley to the west and the low lying fenlands to the east. It is a gentle, undulating landscape with a series of ridges and valleys formed by streams flowing east from the higher ground to the fens. Small villages lie scattered across the area, mainly in the sheltered valleys, but it remains a sparsely populated rural landscape.

It is a modern-day agricultural landscape dominated by large-scale arable farmland. Increased mechanization has led to the removal of many hedgerows and the amalgamation of fields into larger more economically productive units. Where field boundaries remain, the hedges are often trimmed out of existence, their presence further diminished by the loss of elm trees to disease. Larger farms have led to the construction of large modern storage units which now dominate the landscape in much the same way that church spires would have done in the past.

The area is notable for its heavy clay soils which are particularly favourable for growing wheat and barley. This is reflected in the description of the area as the Western Claylands[1] by the local authority and the epithet often applied to the neighbouring village of Lutton as *Mucky Lutton*[2]. Whether the Jacksons living here in the past would recognize this modern landscape is uncertain, but they would surely be familiar with the heavy clay soils on which they toiled for most of their working lives.

As well as modern agricultural practices, de-population has also changed the nature of the landscape. The number of people living in Washingley has declined dramatically from around a hundred at the start of the eighteenth century to just a handful today[3]. There are now only a few cottages and farms spread out along two country lanes – Washingley Lane, which forms a dog-leg running east-west, and Bullock Road, which runs north-south along higher ground to the west. The sense of isolation is further enhanced by the fact that

FACING PAGE
1.1 The upside down map of 1761 (on a north-south alignment with north at the top of the page). This shows Washingley Hall Estate and the 'dog leg' of Washingley Lane running through the centre.

there is no church, village centre or any other focal point of rural life. Visiting the area for the first time, it is easy to miss the village altogether – if it was not for the road and village signs. The modern day visitor is hard-pressed to imagine a community living and working in the area for successive generations.

But what is still as evident today as it would have been for previous generations, are the physical remains of the area's rich medieval past. Although there are few signs of prehistoric and Roman settlement – perhaps due to the dense woodlands and heavy clay soils – there are many remains of medieval occupation throughout the area. Growing population pressures and advances in farming techniques during the early medieval period meant that many settlements were established during this time. This influence is still highly visible and in addition to ancient settlements and field patterns there are many sites of medieval manors, fishponds, woodlands, hedges and ridge and furrow patterns.

1.2 Display board illustrating the possible site of Washingley Castle.

It is no surprise therefore to find that Washingley was recorded as a small Anglo-Saxon farming community, known as Wasinglei, in the Domesday Survey in the 11th century[4]. There are earthworks consisting of a possible motte and bailey in what would have been the centre of the village which may have been the site of the manor house recorded in the 13th century. Rather ambitiously, Cambridgeshire County Council describe this as the site of Washingley Castle, but admit that the earthworks could just as easily have been created at a much later date to add interest to the garden of the Hall subsequently built on the site. The positioning of a display board, some 50 metres south of Washingley Lane and only visible to the keenest explorer, only adds to the sense of reluctance to promote too strongly the notion of Washingley and its castle.

There are further earthworks to the north of Washingley Lane, consisting of ponds, banks and platforms, which represent the site of a deserted medieval village, which has Scheduled Monument status. Saville (1992) suggests that in the early 14th century it was a village of over 200 people and large enough to support a church and a resident priest. Like many other settlements in the area, it declined rapidly during and after the Black Death, which swept across the country in 1348. By the middle of the following century the population was down to around 60 and the Bishop of Lincoln directed that the Church be closed and villagers should resort to using Lutton as their mother church. This could have been the end of Washingley had not the Manor passed by marriage to the Apreece family[5] who moved their seat to the village in 1522 where they stayed for the next 350 years.

The last surviving member of the Apreece family died unmarried in 1842 and the Estate was eventually bought by the Earl of Harrington who remodeled the house and created a new Washingley Hall. After passing through various hands it was bought by Lord Cobham in 1934 who demolished it shortly afterwards. All that remains today are the stone pillars surmounted by eagles which formed the original entranceway to the house. These now form a rather grand – and somewhat incongruous – entrance to what is a now a functional modern farmhouse and buildings. The layout of the drive and garden walls can still be seen in the grass along with the kitchen garden to the east of the house. The fishponds are now beneath mature trees which would once have formed the pleasure gardens[6].

In the Huntingdon Record Office, there is a large painted map of the estate, produced by T. Lewis in 1765, containing one of the few remaining images of the Hall and landscaped gardens. The plan is strangely annotated upside down, so that when laid out according to the alignment of the text, the direction of north is downwards. This is disorientating to the reader and also mysterious, especially given the amount of effort that must have gone into producing the map. Why deliberately annotate a map upside down, unless the cartographer made a mistake and the map was rejected which might explain why it survives today.

In the north-west corner of Washingley parish are the ruins of Osgerton, a manor granted to the Knights Templar in the 12th century. This became an important location in the Middle Ages as part of an alternative north-south routeway alongside the fens. Christopher Taylor[7] has illustrated how the direct route following the Roman Road of Ermine Street appears to have been abandoned, perhaps after other bridges or culverts failed. Travellers may have sought alternative and drier routes along the higher ground. Taylor suggests that Osgerton must have formed an important part of that route, now known as the Bullock Road, as it was included on the 1360 Gough Map showing principle routes in Britain.

The Jacksons in Washingley

Just when the Jacksons entered into this story of medieval England remains uncertain. The earliest recorded Jackson living in the area is Henricus (Jacsonn) who married Anne Cockerill in 1591 at Caldicot. Whether Henricus was the first in the Jackson line, or even in the direct line at all, remains uncertain – not least because of the fragmented nature of the records for Washingley – but it seems likely that he would have been related in some way to the later Jacksons.

My first direct recorded ancestor is Joseph Jackson who was born in Washingley in 1766. He married Elizabeth and their third child, William born in 1804, was my great-great grandfather. William married Ruth Tansley from the nearby village of Haddon in 1833 and their third child, also called William and born in 1837, was my great grandfather. William married Elizabeth Moulton from Washingley in 1862 and their third child was my grandfather Thomas, born in 1867. Thomas married Emma Wallis from nearby Ashton just outside Oundle in 1895, now better known as the home of the World Conker Championship. Their eldest son, Thomas my father, was born the following year in November 1896.

All my direct ancestors worked as agricultural labourers and must have been familiar figures on the heavy clay soils in the exposed and unforgiving landscape. They all lived in the village, either in various cottages in Washingley Lane or in the Bullock Road. But this line of the Jackson family was not alone in Washingley. There were many other Jacksons living in the village at this time and in many of the neighbouring parishes of Folksworth, Lutton, Caldecot and Stilton. During most of the 1800s, a quarter of the inhabitants of Washingley, which averaged around 100–120 people at the time, either had the Jackson name or were related by marriage on the female side. Again, almost all of the working Jacksons were recorded as agricultural labourers.

Like most of the rest of the rural population the Jackson family had little or no formal education and were unable to read and write. There was of course little opportunity for the rural poor to gain an education and although there was a Sunday School and also a so-called 'dame school'[8] in Lutton in the 1850s, it was not until the opening of the Church of England School in 1876 that all children in Washingley and Lutton had an opportunity for schooling. However, as attendance was only voluntary and cost a penny per child per week, it is not surprising that the school remained under its capacity of 40 children until 1891 when the Elementary Education Act resulted in the provision of free education, and attendance surprisingly rose to 60.

By 1862 when my great grandfather, William, married Elizabeth Moulton, neither he nor his brother John were able to sign the marriage register and had to make their mark instead. William and Elizabeth's son, my grandfather Thomas born in 1867, was the first of my direct ancestors to be literate and by the time of his marriage in 1895 had a very neat and legible hand. It is unlikely that his parents could have afforded to pay for his education and as he would have been too old to benefit from free provision, he presumably learned

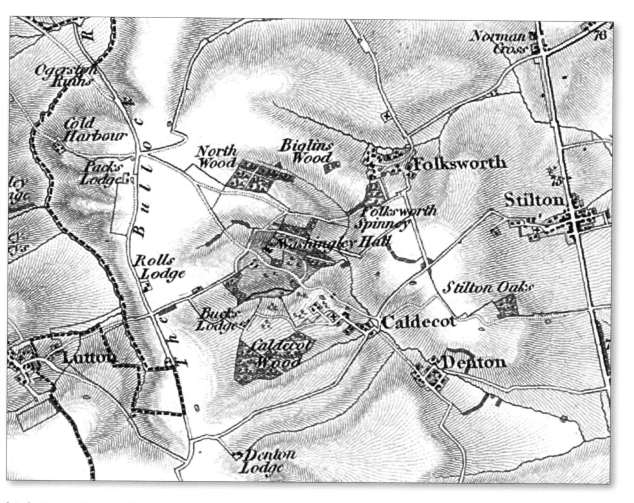

his letters at home, either from his mother Elizabeth or his younger brothers and sisters. My father Thomas was the first to benefit from the provision of compulsory free education for all.

The Jacksons were employed directly on the Washingley Estate – and by the various tenant farmers managing the land – and were probably also involved in cattle droving along the Bullock Road. Huge herds of cattle, sometimes as many as 200,000 per year[9], were driven along this drove road during the 1700s and 1800s on their way from Scotland and the North of England to the thriving markets in London. Drovers often used this route to avoid paying the tolls charged by turnpike authorities and enterprising farmers in the area provided overnight and watering facilities. This also provided an opportunity for local graziers[10] who purchased cattle in the springtime, to fatten them up over the summer before driving them to the London market in the autumn. The coming of the railways in the later part of the nineteenth century brought a rapid end to this practice and the loss of a vital source of income for local farm workers.

1.4 Mid-19th century map showing Washingley and Lutton bisected by the Bullock Road and the county boundary.

To what extent my immediate ancestors were involved in cattle droving remains unknown, as census records and parish registers from the time simply record most agricultural workers as labourers. It is tempting however to see some link – whether practical or psychological – between the Jackson family recorded as living and working on the Bullock Road and my father's subsequent occupation as cow-herd and stockman.

John Clare

Washingley is, of course, only 15 miles or so to the south of Helpston, home of the so-called 'Northamptonshire peasant poet' John Clare. Clare was born in 1793 and spent much of his working life as a seasonal agricultural labourer – as well as being a pot-boy, gardener and lime burner. He rose to fame following the publication of his Poems *Descriptive of Early Life and Society* in 1820 before his subsequent decline and admission to the Lunatic Asylum in Northampton in 1841, where he died in 1863.

Clare's description of the beauty of the countryside and the changing nature of the seasons celebrates the nature of rural life at this time. But this was also a time of massive change in the countryside due to the effects of the Agricultural Revolution and the Enclosure Act and Clare was deeply distressed by what he saw as the destruction of a centuries old way of life. Many of the sentiments he expresses would have been familiar to those fellow agricultural labourers some 15 miles down the Great North Road in Washingley.

In his excellent account of Clare's life, the biographer Jonathan Bate recalls a letter that Clare sent from Northampton Asylum to his son in 1849, asking about the welfare of many of the families he had known from Helpston, including 'Frank Jackson and His Wife'[11]. By 1851, the answer would have been 'not very well', because by then, Frank and his wife Catherine, both in their seventies, were recorded as paupers in the village. Whether they, or their neighbours, John and Elizabeth Jackson were related to the Jacksons from Washingley remains unknown.

Less well known is the fact that Clare also had a keen interest in antiquities and his musings on the past and the mortality (and immortality) of man are reflected in many of his poems. In the early 1820s he became close friends with Edmund Artis a local antiquarian and archaeologist. In 1821 Artis unearthed a Roman mosaic at Castor and subsequently spent many years exploring and mapping the Roman town of Durobrivae. He published a collection of engraved plates illustrating his discoveries, entitled The *Durobrivae of Antoninus*, and was made a Fellow of the Society of Antiquities in recognition of his work. Clare himself found fragments of Roman pottery in Oxley Wood, just outside Helpston, and Artis excavated the site and discovered a Roman villa. Clare later wrote a report on the discovery for the local Stamford Mercury.

Although there is no known direct link between Washingley and Clare, a tenuous connection has been made by the modern-day author and writer

Iain Sinclair. In 1841, Clare had run away from the High Beech Asylum in Epping Forest, Essex and walked the 80 miles back to his home in Northborough in the hope of seeing his first love, Mary Joyce, who, unknown to him had died three years earlier. In 2000 Sinclair retraced Clair's three day walk from Epping Forest to Northborough, just outside Helpston[12].

Sinclair's trip was partly inspired by his wife Anna's belief that her family, the Hadmans, were related to Clare. Anna Hadman's family had lived in Glinton, the adjacent village to Helpston and where Clare went to school.

1.5 Engraving from *The Durobrivae of Antoninus* showing E. A. Artis conducting a Roman excavation.

Sinclair discovered that the early Hadmans all came from Caldicot, the hamlet adjacent to Washingley, and that Robert Hadman, Anna's great-great-grandfather was born in Washingley in 1808. Sinclair trawls the 19th century Estate records for Washingley but fails to find any reference to the Hadmans, because – just like the Jacksons – they were all agricultural labourers and beneath the level that produced recordable revenue for the estate. So although the Hadmans and Jacksons would certainly have known each other in Washingley, any familial connection with Clare remains a matter of conjecture.

Clare's lament for the lost countryside of his youth was partly caused by growing rural poverty during the first half of the nineteenth century. The Napoleonic wars and rising food prices had forced many agricultural workers to leave the countryside and seek work elsewhere, especially in the growing number of factories being established in towns.

1.6 Reconstruction of Roman mosaic based on fragment discovered by John Clare.

While some members of the extended Jackson family left Washingley over the years – for work and other purposes – it was not until my grandfather left in 1899 that a member of my direct family had moved permanently away from the village. Whether this was ever intended to be as permanent as it turned out to be is unknown, but it would not have been easy leaving the people, houses and landscape that the family had known all this time.

Paula Maybery

CHAPTER TWO

Home and Away in Southwick

"I long for scenes where man has never trod
A place where woman never smiled or wept
There to abide with my Creator God
And sleep as I in childhood sweetly slept,
Untroubling and untroubled where I lie
The grass below, above, the vaulted sky."

John Clare, I Am

Arrival in Southwick

After leaving Washingley, Thomas and Emma moved east towards the wolds, first to Yaxley and then on to Whittlesey, where they lived at Whype. They later moved back to Yaxley again, Thomas finding work as an agricultural labourer wherever he could. The younger Thomas soon had a sister, Jane Elizabeth, born in Yaxley in 1900, followed by a brother Samuel Wallis born in Whittlesea in 1902. Once back in Yaxley, further children followed at frequent intervals; Albert in 1905, Harry and Georgina in 1907, Georgina in 1909 and Lucy in 1910.

It was shortly after the birth of Lucy, that a new opportunity presented itself, across the border in Southwick, Northamptonshire. Samuel Wallis, Emma's father was foreman and shepherd for the Capron family of Southwick Hall and when additional farm labourers were required, Samuel immediately thought of his daughter and their young family living just ten miles away in Yaxley. This was a good move for the Jackson family, because it not only provided jobs for both the elder and the younger Thomas, who was now 14, but it also provided the growing family with a bigger cottage at Southwick Grange.

Southwick is a small delightful village nestling neatly in the Nene Valley just three miles north of Oundle. It consists of a single main street, with cottages built from local Collyweston stone and slate. It is dominated at one end by Southwick Hall and the adjacent church of St Mary's. There is evidence that the village had a thriving iron-smelting industry in the 10th century and a medieval stone hall dating from the mid-13th century may have been a manse owned by St. Marys Priory, Huntingdon[13].

The Hall was built in the 1300s by Richard Knyvett who was a prominent wool merchant in the area and whose son, Sir John, was Lord Chancellor of Edward III. In the 1440s the house was sold to John Lynn who had married Joan Knyvett. His son, George Lynn, was responsible for rebuilding the house. He was one of the eight bannerol-bearers at the funeral of Mary Queen of Scots at Peterborough Cathedral after her execution, and there is a legend that

FACING PAGE
2.1 Painting of Southwick Hall by Paula Maybery which captures the peace and timeless quality of the setting.
www. paulamayberyartgallery.com

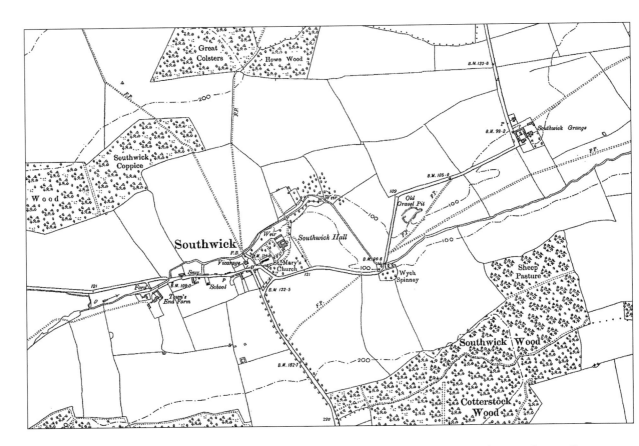

2.2 Southwick at the start of the 20th century. The Jackson family lived in a cottage at Southwick Grange (top right).

the burial certificate is walled up somewhere in the house. George Lynne was connected by marriage to Walter Raleigh, who is reputed to have visited the house. The Hall was then bought by a London solicitor, George Capron in 1841, who had previously acquired the manor of Stoke Doyle. The Capron family have lived in the Hall ever since.

The move to Southwick was a big change for the Jacksons as life in the village revolved around the Capron family and the Hall. This would initially have been daunting for the shy younger Thomas who had little personal or social experience outside the close agricultural community. However, along with the rest of the family, he soon began to play an active part in church and village life. This was aided no doubt by the impact that a large young family can have on a small community, because Thomas and Emma soon had 10 children all under the age of fifteen, having finally added Rebecca and Francis to their growing family. They lived just outside of the village at Grange Cottage, which had previously been occupied by just Samuel and his wife, so fitting 2 adults and 10 young children into the same space must have been something of a challenge. Years later, when Emma died at 60, the doctor is reported to have said *'she was simply worn out'*. It is not hard to understand why.

In addition to the Hall and church, life at Southwick – especially for the menfolk – also revolved around the local inn, the Shuckburgh Arms, situated on the main street just a stone's throw from the church. This had also been acquired by George Capron in the 1840s when he purchased the estate and he named it after his cousin, the Reverend John Shuckburgh, who was related to the Lynne family. The Inn was original run by Henry Pick and his wife Harriett, who subsequently went on to be farmers in the village. In the 1890s it was taken over by ex-butcher Herbert Wallis from Ashton, and his wife Ellen, who was related to Samuel and Emma Wallis. In the early years of the new century, shortly before the Jackson's moved to the village, the inn was run by William Monk and his wife Fanny, who had previously been coachman and domestic servants for the Caprons.

The First World War

Within this ready-made close knit community, enclosed by the wooded slopes of Southwick and Glapthorn woods, life could not have been further removed from the years spent travelling around the exposed, bleak landscape of the fens. But their new found life was to change dramatically with the outbreak of the First World War in 1914. Although this did not have any immediate effect on the Jacksons as a family, as the younger Thomas was only 17, just too young to enlist, and his father was 47, just too old; Lord Kitchener's pleas for voluntary enlistment would have featured heavily in all their thoughts during the coming months.

By the Spring of 1915 when it became clear to the Government that voluntary recruitment was not going to provide the numbers required, it introduced the National Registration Act, followed by the Derby Scheme, to encourage enlistment. The War Office subsequently announced that voluntary enlistment would be replaced by conscription and that the last day for voluntary registration was 15th December 1915.

Just a few days before, on 11th December, and now just 19, Thomas and his friend David Monk, also 19 and a fellow farmworker and son of William Monk, the landlord of the Shuckburgh Arms, made the three mile journey together to Oundle for their Attestation. Here they both swore the oath and enlisted for service in front of Justice Smith of Oundle. The paperwork and medical examinations were completed and they were sent back to their homes and jobs to wait to be called up.

At the time, neither would have presented much of an obvious physical threat to the German forces; Thomas was just five foot five inches and barely weighed eight stone, whilst David was a little bigger at five foot seven. Full of excitement and enthusiasm they returned proudly displaying the grey armband with the red crown to show that they were volunteers.

The following months would have been nerve-wracking as they and their families monitored the progress of the war and awaited the inevitable call-up. David Monk was mobilized first, joining the Royal Garrison Artillery in May 1916 and being posted almost immediately to France. He served on the

Western Front for over two years, but was sadly killed in action near Yypes on 26th July 1918.

Thomas was mobilized in August 1916 when he joined the Northamptonshire Regiment but was not posted to France until later that year, embarking from Folkestone to Boulogne on 10th December 1916. Thomas survived the two remaining years of the War as in Infrantryman on the Western Front. His postcards home reveal his love for his family in Southwick but understandably, say nothing about the experience or conditions he was facing. We do know that he was admitted to hospital three times during this period; in June 1917, for paroxysmal haemoglobinuria[14]; in April 1918 when he was wounded in action with a scalp injury, and two months later for an unknown complaint. Despite this Thomas survived, his only misdemeanor occurred three weeks after the end of the War in November 1918 when he was confined to barracks for five days for yawning on patrol. Finally he embarked for England on 17th February 1919 and was demobilized from Purfleet three days later.

One of the few remaining records of Thomas' wartime service is a thank you note from Brigadier General of the Northamptonshire Regiment that he was given when demobilized. This contains a sharp reminder of the popular attitude towards the War at that time, with Thomas being reminded that ..."*You have played the game, go on playing it, and all will be well with the great Empire which you have helped to save*". Some game, with almost 3 million British servicemen being killed, injured or reported missing during the conflict[15].

2.3 Thank you note from the Northamptonshire Regiment given to Thomas on his demobilisation.

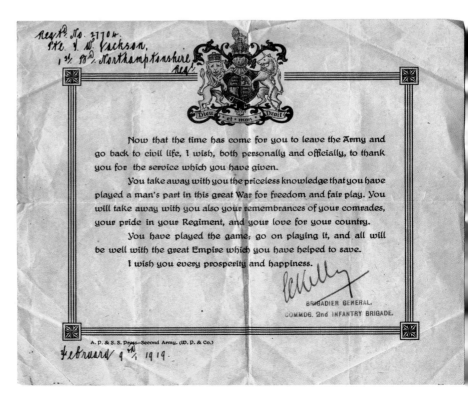

Back in Southwick

Like all returning servicemen, Thomas' joy at returning to his life and loved ones in Southwick must have been overwhelming, but constantly tempered by his experiences in France and the reminder of David Monk and his bereaved family at the Shuckburgh Arms. He returned to his old job as stockman working for the Bonser family. He kept his thoughts to himself and rarely spoke about his feelings or experiences during the War preferring the time he spent alone in the fields with the cows.

Thomas was soon persuaded to join the Southwick Brass Band, although where he obtained any musical ability (if he had any) remains uncertain. This was no small commitment, however, as all members were required to pay a shilling upon receiving their instrument and contribute two-pence a week towards the

2.4 Southwick Brass Band, 1920s, back row left to right: S. Jackson, A. Reed, S. Wallis, T. Jackson, W. Rowell; front row left to right: T. Kerfoot, H. Wallis, H. Jackson, A. Jackson, J. Reed (almost the Jackson Five).

upkeep of the Band. The Band had been formed in 1895 with George Capron as President but had disbanded at the outbreak of the War. It was reformed after the War and famously performed to welcome Colonel Capron back from India in 1921.

The surviving Rules of the Band provide a fascinating insight into life and expected behaviour at that time. For example, Rule 9 stipulates that: *"On practice nights every Bandsman must endeavour to be present and conduct himself in an honourable gentlemanly way, by obeying all authority to his utmost, trying to set up a noble example, doing his best to help in any entertainments, or whatever the Officers think fit for the support of the Band"*. And Rule 11 states that: *"No bad language shall be used in the practice room, but quietness and good behaviour must abound there as is necessary to become good musicians"*. The Bandsmen were also forbidden from blowing their instrument in the street or causing annoyance to anyone – presumably to discourage unruly Bandsmen from running riot through the street of Southwick.

A Southwick Wedding

Playing in the band expanded Thomas' social life and his connections within Southwick and the surrounding villages. It also led to him meeting, and subsequently courting, Katie Hill, then the new chief cook at Southwick Hall. Katie was born in the fenlands at Crowland, just north of Peterbough in 1899, the daughter of Elizabeth Hill from nearby Deeping St Nicholas. It is uncertain who Katie's father was but she took the name of Katie Dolby when her mother married James Dolby and moved to Downham Market in Norfolk just a few years after she was born. Katie was the eldest and played a key role in the upbringing of her two half brothers and four half sisters. This led to her skill in the kitchen and she was subsequent employed as chief cook at Southwick Hall. Sarah Elizabeth Hill and Joseph Hill, her aunt and uncle, were living at Oundle at the time and it was during a visit to them that she obtained her job with the Caprons at Southwick Hall. She then reverted back to her original name of Katie Hill.

Little did Katie, or her mother Elizabeth know, that their humble position belied a more noble pedigree. Elizabeth's father James Hill, an agricultural labourer from Langtoft, Lincolnshire, had married Anne Blackham, from Beeston, Nottinghamshire, the daughter of William Blackham, a journeyman blacksmith. The Blackham family had lived in the West Midlands area for seven generations and were descended directly from Sir John Cooke of Gidea Hall, Essex. Sir John's father-in-law was William Saunders who had married Jane Spencer in 1501. Jane was the daughter of Sir John Spencer of Wormleighton Hall, Warwickshire, and was of course a member of the noble Spencer family who subsequently acquired Althorpe Hall and a direct link to the future king of England.

So it is only with a partial tongue in the check that Katie Hill, chief cook at Southwick Hall, might have been introduced as a direct descendent of nobility Any knowledge of her lineage would have had little practical effect on Katie's life, as she was far too sensible to have followed the example set by Thomas Hardy's Durbeyfield[16]. But it would have appealed to her sense of humour – and it was certainly one of Life's Little Ironies – that her and Thomas were destined to spend the rest of their lives in service beholden to those deemed to be of higher social standing than themselves.

But none of this would have been on my mother Katie's mind, when she married Thomas Jackson, her own knight in shining armour at Southwick Church in 1925. There were joyful scenes in the rural churchyard with much celebration amongst the villagers, fellow 'downstairs' members of the Capron household and the (many) Jackson siblings, all accompanied by the remaining members of the Brass Band. Thomas was immensely proud – as Katie was quite a catch – (even though he only knew the half of it), but he was rather embarrassed at being the centre of so much attention and rather longed to be back in the solitude of the fields with his cows. The churchyard at Southwick remains a very peaceful and tranquil setting – virtually unchanged since that day – and it is fitting that both Thomas and Katie are buried there along with other members of the Jackson family.

Although Thomas' mother, Emma, was to die a few years later in her early sixties, the elder Thomas lived until he was 89. He remained an active and well-known figure in the village well into his eighties – easily recognized by his dapper dress sense and twirly moustache – and was often to be seen walking the three miles to Oundle and back every day to keep fit.

A Stoke Doyle Birth

Just a year after their marriage, life was to change again for Thomas and Katie when farmer Bonser insisted they move to Stoke Doyle, a village four miles to the south of Southwick, to work on land he had recently acquired. Although also set in beautiful rolling countryside, Stoke Doyle was an unusual village at that time because it consisted simply of a row of 14 terraced houses lining the only road through the village, together with three farmhouses, a church, rectory and public house.

2.5 Stoke Doyle 1929 my first photo shoot.

Thomas and Katie were provided with the end house in the row (Number 14), in a particularly convenient position opposite the school house and next to the village pub. Whether this location – perfectly juxtaposed between the pleasures of the book and the beer – provided portents of my future is uncertain, but it was here, on 20th February 1928 – exactly nine years to the day after Thomas left the Army – that I was born.

CHAPTER THREE

The Early Years

"Little Trotty Wagtail, he waddled in the mud,
And left his little footmarks, trample where he would.
He waddled in the water-pudge, and waggle went his tail,
And chirrup up his wings to dry upon the garden rail."

John Clare, Little Trotty Wagtail

Growing up in Stoke Doyle and Aldwincle

We lived at Stoke Doyle for the first eight years of my life, with only the death of my grandmother Emma in 1933, disturbing a peaceful rural upbringing. It was the same year that I started my school life, and despite living so close (or perhaps because of this) it was with some trepidation that I crossed the road on that first school day. Re-visiting the school today, it is easy to recall those early sentiments as, from the front at least, it remains virtually unchanged. Only the modern rear extension with the proverbial satellite dish betrays the fact that it is now a twentieth-first century home.

Not that anyone would mistake it for a school building today because it must have been one of the smallest schools in the country. There was only one classroom and the average attendance was less than 10 pupils. For much of the

FACING PAGE
3.1 Painting by Mikki Longley. of shop in Aldwincle owned by F. W. Watts & Son since 1934.
www.mikkilongley.com

3.2 Stoke Doyle school today.

3.3 Children from Stoke Doyle including Stanley Beesley (front left) and myself (front right) being held down by unknown female.

time there were only two boys in the school, myself and a fellow pupil Stanley Beesley, whose family was originally from Aldwincle. I spent a lot of time with Stanley in the surrounding fields and on the local rubbish tip which was a popular spot for youngsters of that age. I remember this being particularly exciting when the tip caught fire underneath (much to my parents' horror).

Surprisingly for such a small village, Stoke Doyle had its own occasional cricket team, and the highlight was watching my father open the batting for the village side. He adopted the same unfussy methodical approach to cricket as to the rest of his life, and rarely can the epithet 'Stonewall' Jackson have been more accurately deployed. In much later life, the Northamptonshire and England batsman, David Steele, would bring back fond memories of 'Stonewall's' gallant defence on a turning Stoke Doyle wicket.

3.4 With my younger brother Ken. at Stoke Doyle in 1938.

I was soon joined in Stoke Doyle by a brother Ken and sister Margaret. Life in the village revolved around the family – the teapot was always on and the door was open to family and friends. There were frequent family sing songs around the piano and I remember the big celebration at the coronation of King George in 1936.

The highlight of the week was always Saturdays when I walked the one and a half miles to Oundle with my parents. The small town of Oundle lies almost midway between Southwick and Stoke Doyle and it was the main market place for both villages between the wars. It was then, and still is, one of the most attractive and historic towns in the county, with many fine stone built Georgian buildings, including the famous public school which dominates much of the town. At that time I was far less interested in the town's architectural qualities than in the opportunity it provided to visit the shops and market and to hopefully bump into friends from neighbouring villages.

Towards the end of the 1930s I was shaken out this idyllic, but rather isolated rural life when the family moved to Aldwincle, a larger village three miles to the west. Farmer Bonser had acquired additional land in the village and told my father that we would have to move in order to keep his job. This was exciting as our possessions were loaded on the farm wagon and we made the short journey to our new village.

At Aldwincle, we again lived in a cottage directly opposite the school, which was, in this case, in the grounds of St Peter's church in the centre of the village. The excitement of the move was short-lived however, as my new school was much bigger (it could hardly have been smaller) and some of the boys were bullies, which I had not been used to in the tranquility of Stoke Doyle.

CHURCH AND SCHOOL. ALDWINCLE. THRAPSTON   LILYWHITE COPYRIGHT HALIFAX

3.5 Aldwincle school and church in 1925, directly opposite the cottage where we lived.

This was later made worse by the influx of a large number of evacuees, mainly boys from London. One such lad was Bertie Goodchild, a cheeky cockney who was always up to mischief. On one occasion he put a live mouse in the schoolmistress' desk, an elderly disciplinarian known as Nazzer King. We all waited with baited breath to see the desk opened, and despite threats of increasingly severe punishment, no-one gave Bertie away even though he was still seen as an outsider.

3.6 With my father on a visit to Abington Park, Northampton. The railings were melted down a few years later as a contribution to the war effort.

There were no additional teaching resources to deal with the evacuees with the result that the chances of a good education were strictly limited and it made me appreciate the schooling I had received at Stoke Doyle. Although Nazzer King was highly unpopular with most of the pupils, she had an extensive knowledge and enthusiasm for nature which contributed to my subsequent interest in natural history in later life. My father also encouraged my interest in the natural and historic world, and would, whenever possible organize day trips to interesting local places, including the exciting 'big town' of Northampton that I would subsequently come to know so well.

World War Two

Shortly after moving to Aldwincle, life was further disrupted by the outbreak of the Second World War. When war was declared in September 1939 I was on holiday with my uncle in nearby Corby and we rushed back to Aldwincle thinking that Corby would be bombed straight away. Although we saw a number of German planes fly over the village a few days later it was not until the night of 15 November 1940, when planes were overhead all night as the Germans bombed Coventry, that we experienced the real impact of the war. This was also the night that my youngest brother John was born, (but to what extent the German bombardment contributed to this remains uncertain).

All active men in the village, including Thomas my father, were required to join the Home Guard. They built a look-out platform on top of a tall chestnut tree on the road from Aldwincle to Lowick with a precarious ladder providing access. The men took it in turns to staff the platform and many lonely man-hours were spent up the tree in the belief that they were defending the nation from attack. For our war-effort, the boys were encouraged to kill all the white butterflies to prevent them laying eggs on people's cabbages. Although this all seems so trivial now, in hindsight it was important as it enabled everyone in the community to feel they were making a contribution.

I kept a diary during this time – now sadly lost – and everyday I listened to the radio and recorded the number of planes each side was said to have lost. We were told that the Germans had lost many more planes than we had, and as time progressed I could not understand why the war was not over as the Germans could not possibly have any planes left.

Despite the war, the family was happy in Aldwincle. My father continued to work as a cowman for farmer Bonser, and apart from one holiday a year – when we all went either to Skegness or Hunstanton – he was up at 6 o'clock every morning and worked for twelve hours a day throughout his working life. When not on the farm he was busy on his allotment. Although only a farm-hand he was a well-spoken and intelligent man. Like most women in the village, my mother was an active member of the Mother's Union and the local Conservative Party. I was a member of the church choir, and attended practice regularly throughout the dark winter nights during the black out. A particular friend of the family was Walter Pearson, a garage owner from Burton Latimer. Walter was an eccentric and popular man (having a car may have helped), who, strangely for the time, wore shorts all year round. He had no family and spent much of his time taking us all on outings in his car, which again, in hindsight, may have contributed to my appreciation of this part of the county.

I led a fairly uneventful life as a boy, carrying out menial tasks on the farm such as setting mice traps in the barns and shutting up the hens at night. There was an active boy scouts group in the village and I was proud to be patrol leader on the 'Nightjar' group. We frequently used to play on two mounds in a field known as Henslow meadow, midway between the Aldwincle and Islip. I was puzzled by the mounds at the time but did not know that they were Bronze Age burial mounds – and I had even less of an idea that 25 years later I would excavate the 3000 year old burials that lay beneath the mounds.

A Bricklayers' Apprentice

In common with all the other children, I left Aldwincle school when I was 14 years old. I had always been near to the top in school exams and when I told the headmaster I planned to follow in my father's footsteps – and unknowingly, the rest of my ancestors – and become an agricultural worker he was disappointed. I never did work on the farm however, because a friend who worked in the office of a building firm in the nearby town of Thrapston got me a job as a bricklayer's apprentice. There was a shortage of labour during the war and boys were employed as labourers to the (mainly) grumpy old men who remained. I soon regretted this as I was fairly small for my age and found it very hard work.

One job I had was in the village of Deenethorpe, close to an American air base. A Flying Fortress had crashed in the village and we were required to carry out repairs to the damaged houses. The Fortresses carried out daylight bombing raids over Germany and each morning we watched them take off from the aerodrome and saw the damaged survivors (or at least those planes that had survived) return in the afternoon. It was often a humbling experience that provided a sharp reminder of the reality of the war.

In 1944, an opportunity arose to work in London repairing the building damage caused by German rocket attacks. I saw this as an adventure and escape from the drudgery of work in Thrapston and enthusiastically volunteered. After a few months I was told I was too young to be working in London and would have to return home, but I managed to avoid this by living with my aunt in Tottenham and becoming a London resident. We worked mainly in Hackney carrying out repairs to roofs and windows. The houses were built in one long terrace and when carrying out roof repairs we would erect a ladder at one end of the street and walk along the parapet wall to the other end. It was not unusual for us to repair one street and have to start all over the again the following day due to overnight damage. The work was fairly relaxed and the men often went shopping in the West End during working hours.

Life in London was a far cry from the rural environment I was used to. Although I made few friends I travelled around a lot and got to know the city very well. I frequently went to the cinema and theatre and attended many other events, including being outside Buckingham Palace on both VE day and VJ day. I never felt in any real danger from the rocket attacks, although there was one instance when travelling in an open lorry when a V1 rocket headed straight towards us before veering off at the last moment. A scary but not a common event.

After the War

After the war I returned to the peace and quiet of life in Aldwincle. Like Southwick and Stoke Doyle, Aldwincle is pleasantly situated in the Nene Valley, nestling in a bend in the river, and consists of a straggling main street with rows of attractive cottages built from local stone and slate. It is one of very few villages in the county divided into two parishes, due to the fact that it was originally owned by two different Lords of the Manor. As a result there are two parish churches, St Peter's and All Saints. Aldwincle is also notable for being the home of two distinguished literary figures, John Dryden[17] and Thomas Fuller[18] who were both born in the village, one in each rectory.

3.7 On holiday with brother John in Skegness.

Despite being a small village, it was at that time, a fairly lively place. There were four shops and two inns and with the two churches there always seemed to be

people moving around the place and a lot of children playing outside. Today, it is a much changed place; there are no pubs and only one shop remains, possibly because it is still owned by the same family – the Watts' – that had it sixty years ago. But there are rarely signs of people, and certainly no children outside. Most people only emerge to move briefly between their 4x4s and their sympathetically modernized cottages. There are of course, no more outside toilets and many of the other disadvantages of rural life that we conveniently forget, but I feel our rapid progress towards an improved quality of life has been achieved at the expense of the heart and soul of many rural communities like Aldwincle.

At that time, the village also had its own cricket team and I used to make up the numbers when they were short. For a time I played football for the nearby village of Barnwell, home of the Duke of Gloucester, and there were a number of occasions when I could claim my endeavours on the field were watched – if not necessarily appreciated – by royalty.

The winter of 1947 was notoriously bad. The severe weather began in late January and everything was frozen until mid March. The village was cut off by deep snow and unemployed builders such as myself were employed by the county council to clear a pathway to the nearby village of Thorpe Achurch. There was severe flooding throughout the area when the cold weather was eventually replaced by torrential rain which melted the frozen snow. I soon realized that I had been spoiled by the easy life I had led in London and I was fortunate to be re-employed by my previous boss after the winter when all building workers were laid off.

By the time I was 21, it was clear that opportunities in the local building trade were limited and I decided to seek work further afield. I visited the offices of the big contracting firms in London and obtained work in the town centres of Sheffield and Southampton which were both being rebuilt after the war. I also worked in the new town of Stevenage and on a big civil engineering project at Maple Cross in Hertfordshire.

Meeting Betty

My parents were still living in Aldwincle and it was on one of my visits home in 1949 that I met my future wife, Betty, at a social evening in the village hall. Betty was the only daughter of Arthur Overton from Kettering and his wife Alice Stanley who now lived in Thrapston. Betty was a seamstress in a local clothing factory, and being the only girl alongside her four brothers – Michael, Colin, Barry and Graham – she had a robust and lively sense of humour. Visiting the Overton household at that time was certainly never dull. After a short courtship we were married two years later in Thrapston in 1951.

3.8 Katie Jackson opening the batting at Skegness in 1951 with Betty at first slip, brother John as silly point and Thomas at silly mid on (unsure who was bowling but they must have doubled up as photographer).

3.9 Marriage to Betty with, from left to right, my mother Katie, Colin (Betty's brother behind), Margaret (my sister), my father Thomas, Alice and Stanley Overton.

3.10 With first son Stephen on the beach in 1953.

At the time of our wedding, I was working for Bovis in Northampton, refacing the brickwork on the Marks and Spencer store in Gold Street, so we decided to move to the town. We were soon able to buy our first house in Byron Street, an area known as Poets Corner, (which unknowingly continued the literary tradition from Clare to Dryden etc). We lived in Northampton in various parts of the town for the next fifty years. Betty combined raising a family with a successful dressmaking business working from home. She also got enormous pleasure from teaching dressmaking at adult evening classes, many of which were carried out at the John Clare centre in Northampton. Sadly, Betty died in 2001 just a few weeks before we were due to celebrate our golden wedding anniversary.

Although we had recently moved to Northampton, most of our free time in the 1950s was still spent with our families in the Aldwincle/ Thrapston area, especially following the birth of our first son Stephen in 1952 and daughter Sandra in 1956, when their support was much appreciated. Betty's parents had aquired a number of caravans at Hunstanton where we spent many happy holidays. At that time this involved a cross-country journey of some four hours each way travelling between Northampton and the east coast. This was always an adventure, especially the time the brakes failed on the car in Kings Lynn and we careered down the hill coming to rest calmly in the centre of a conveniently placed roundabout.

The Building Trade

For the following 14 years I was a self-employed brickwork contractor in Northampton and carried out work throughout the town, especially in the Abington and Kingsley areas. Much of my work was for a local builder called Holton, but I also carried out more prestigious projects including work for building societies, the police and the construction of two Mormon churches.

In 1951 I took over a small building contract and from then on employed between one and ten people depending on the work. I was always paid by the number of bricks laid, so it became vital to organise and plan the work to make the best use of the people available. I believe I continued this approach in my archaeological work, and always tried to plan ahead to make the best use of the resources available. For many years, I employed a labourer called George Sankey who never used a hod and carried bricks and mortar up and down a ladder all day on his head. George liked his beer and had a reputation as a *'ten pints a night man'* but in all the years he worked for me he was never known to drop a thing. In his own way, George also provided a valuable lesson on the importance of productivity and hard work for producing results – irrespective of how this was achieved – which was to become another important guide to me when managing archaeological excavations in future years.

Back in Aldwincle my father became ill and was forced to retire. He had worked for farmer Bonser all his life and was understandably devastated when the family was forced to leave the tied cottage that was their home. They left the village and moved to the town of Burton Latimer where my brother Ken lived. Thomas never recovered his health and died in 1969. Katie moved back to Islip, a village near Aldwincle, where she lived until her death in the late 1970s.

3.11 The last photograph of the Jackson family together at Burton Latimer in the mid-1960s shortly before Thomas died, from left to right, myself, Ken, Thomas, John, Katie and Margaret.

By the mid 1960s I had plenty of building work in Northampton, and a young family to support (Christopher being born in 1966). But other interests were beginning to dominate my life. What had started as a mild interest in the history and archaeology of the county was turning into an obsession that was to dominate the rest of my life.

I was unaware at the time that I was the first member of the Jackson family in six generations not to work on the land. But soil must run somewhere in the Jackson blood, because, while previous members of the family worked the earth to provide for the future, I was destined to work the earth in a different way; in a way that would hopefully help us better understand our past.

PART TWO

A Professional Archaeologist

CHAPTER FOUR

1960s: The Early Period

"Here where I stand thy voice breathes from the ground
A buried tale of sixteen hundred years,
And many a Roman fragment, littered round,
In each new-rooted mole-hill reappears."

John Clare, The Triumphs of Time

If it is possible to identify a single moment in time that acts as a pivotal turning point in one's life, it was my decision in 1961 to attend a Workers Educational Association course in archaeology in Northampton. My rural upbringing had encouraged a keen interest in local history and the natural environment but I had no formal education or training in the subject. I did, however, have a growing desire to find out more about the past and, overcoming any apprehension about the academic requirements for the course, I enthusiastically enrolled for the 12 weekly sessions.

Miss Norma Whitcombe, who had responsibility for archaeology at Northampton Museum, ran the course and encouraged all the students to start fieldwalking in their local area. As most weekends were spent with family in the Thrapston/Adwincle area I began in a ploughed field just outside the village of Titchmarsh between the road and railway line. I could not have made a more encouraging start and collected a large quantity of pottery and other artifacts from the field. My delight at presenting them to Miss Whitcombe was somewhat tempered by her reply *"Oh dear Mr Jackson, don't pick all the pottery up as we will never know where the site is"*.

This did nothing to curb my enthusiasm for fieldwalking, although it did teach me the importance of archaeological context at an early stage. I purchased a set of excellent black and white aerial photographs of the Aldwincle area from Dr St Joseph at Cambridge University which helped me target my fieldwalking on sites revealed by crop marks in the area.

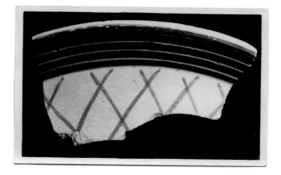

4.1 One of the first pieces of Roman pottery I found at Titchmarsh and recorded as "reddish-brown lattice-work painted on cream base found on 12 February 1961".

Titchmarsh – My First Excavation

In 1962 part of the site at Titchmarsh was being destroyed by gravel quarrying and Norma Whitcombe excavated a number of Roman burials in advance of the quarrying. The graves overlay features containing Iron Age pottery and there were deep ditches exposed in the quarry face with coin evidence that supported a site of this period. This was my first exposure to archaeological excavation and

4.2 My first real excavation at Titchmarsh in 1962, revealing the Roman road in the quarry edge.

to the importance of stratification for understanding and dating the sequence of past human activity.

Later that year, on the same site, I carried out the first 'dig' of my own along with David Johnston, a teacher at Northampton Grammar School. The Roman Gartree Road, which was a major route between Godmanchester and Leicester ran across the floodplain of the River Nene near the Titchmarsh field. We opened some trenches on the line of the road and found some metalling overlying later Roman features.

Nearby, the central area of the small Roman town was being deep ploughed for the first time and gravel quarrying was encroaching on the area from the west. I started watching the area and observed many deep ditches and pits destroyed by the quarrying. In addition to the usual pottery and occupational debris brought to the surface by the deep ploughing, I found part of a stone capital in the area which suggests there was a building of some status in the town. Soon after, when a nearby stream was being cleaned out to improve drainage, a Roman boundary stone with two surviving letters was brought up from the stream bed. Despite my excitement I was overdressed to carry the stone away and a long way from the car so I turned it faced down and planned to collect it later. I was very disappointed to return and find it gone, but when the stream was again cleaned out later it resurfaced and together with Mr Terry, the curator of Northampton Museum, we managed to get the stone safely back to the museum.

Involvement with Local Archaeological Societies

Greatly encouraged by my initial activities, I started to read whatever archaeological material I could find and attend courses whenever possible. I went on a number of residential courses at Knuston Hall where we had practical and experienced tutors such as Dr Dennis Harding, Philip Ratz, Peter Reynolds and Graham Webster. I also attended courses run by the Oxford University Extra-Mural Department where I remember meeting a much younger Mick Aston, now of Time Team fame.

I also started to play an active role in local society affairs. At that time, most archaeological work was carried out by local societies of enthusiastic amateurs and volunteers. There I was fortunate to come under the influence of Richard 'Dick' Hollowell, who was undoubtedly the 'father' of Northamptonshire archaeology in the twentieth century. Dick, a market gardener from Cogenhoe, had walked field after field looking for archaeological evidence and, supported by his own aerial photographs, he revolutionised what was known about the distribution of sites in the county. His work was greatly admired by many eminent academics, including Professor Hawkes of Oxford University, who suggested this was what all local societies should be doing.

In 1963, Dick founded the Upper Nene Archaeological Society (UNAS) and shortly afterwards was instrumental in bringing all the societies in the county together to form the Federation of Archaeological Societies in Northamptonshire. This later became the Northamptonshire Archaeological Society (NAS) which, from 1974 has published an annual county journal. Since that time, UNAS and NAS have been at the centre of the amateur side of archaeology in Northamptonshire, and I am extremely proud to have been a member of both.

Back in the sixties I was privileged to be given the role of excavation officer for the newly formed UNAS. Our first excavation involved digging trial trenches in the grounds of Yardley Hastings Manor at the request of the owner. After some initial enthusiasm from members the only person to turn up regularly was Harold Frost an elderly architect from Northampton. I would collect Harold in my car from the town centre after he had wound the clock of All Saints church, and then play a medieval board game with him through most of our lunch breaks.

4.3 Yes, it's definitely a pot. A local 'Animal, Vegetable or Mineral' session in 1964 with (left to right) Harold Frost, myself and Dick Hollowell.

In 1965 we were notified by a local builder that they had revealed some archaeological features in house foundations at Martins Lane in Hardingstone. This was highly unusual at that time – pre-dating the introduction of developer responsibilities by about 30 years – and we subsequently discovered that pottery was being made on the site in the 1st century AD.

Upton – My First Professional Excavation

In the same year, a dual carriageway was constructed on the A45 to the west of Northampton, and, in the process, some pits were revealed just to the west of Upton church. We organized a rescue excavation and while excavating these Iron Age pits, a service trench dug alongside the new carriageway exposed a collection of Anglo-Saxon loomweights. We enlarged the section of the trench and found that the loomweights lay on the floor of a well-preserved Saxon weaving shed.

4.4 Anglo-Saxon loomweights found at Upton.

We invited Dennis Harding from Oxford University to visit the initial excavation, following which he wrote to J.R.C Hamilton, the Chief Inspector at the Ministry of Works, stressing the importance of, and threat to, the site. Dr Harding re-visited the site, along with Mr Robertson-MacKay, the Inspector

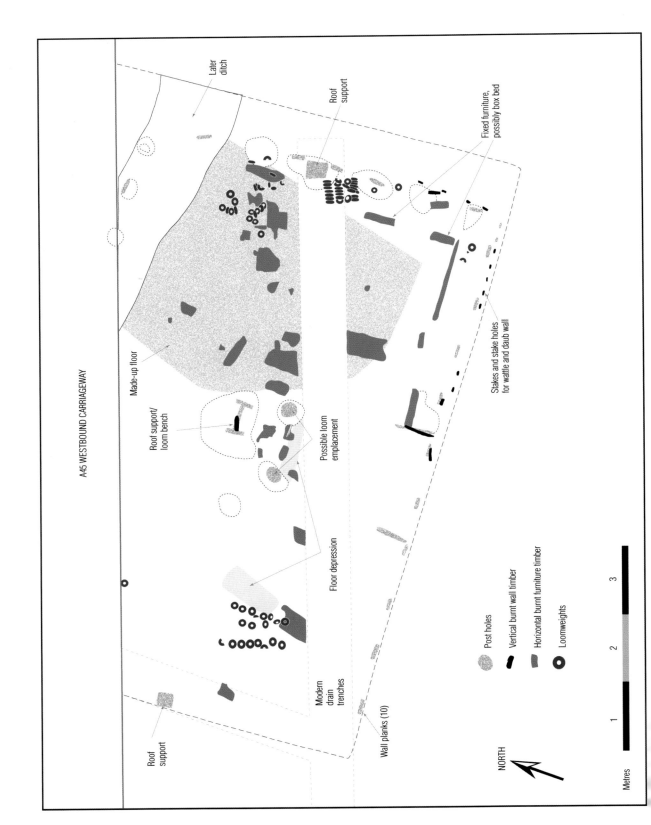

A45 WESTBOUND CARRIAGEWAY

Later ditch

Roof support

Fixed furniture, possibly box bed

Made-up floor

Roof support/ loom bench

Possible loom emplacement

Stakes and stake holes for wattle and daub wall

Floor depression

Modern drain trenches

Wall planks (10)

Roof support

○ Post holes

▬ Vertical burnt wall timber

▬ Horizontal burnt furniture timber

◉ Loomweights

1   2   3

NORTH

Metres

FACING PAGE
4.5 Plan of Anglo-Saxon weaving
shed at Upton.

LEFT
4.6 A photographic session at
Upton.

for Prehistory, and it was agreed that the Ministry of Works would fund a small
full time excavation. I was asked if I was prepared to continue and direct the
work for a month, and although I agreed, I never envisaged a permanent move
to become a full time archaeologist, especially as I had plenty of profitable
building work and the offer of £25 for the month was hardly an incentive. But I
nevertheless accepted and, almost by default, became the first field archaeologist
to be employed in the county. Perhaps the second seminal moment in my
archaeological career (from turning to tipping point).

This was my first 'professional' excavation. It was particularly rewarding as the
building displayed a remarkable combination of the structural features of a
Grubenhaus (sunken building) with the dimensions and plan of a small timber
hall (without partitions). The building contained more than 60 loomweights
and was interpreted as a weaving shed rather than a domestic occupation site.

The structure had been destroyed by fire and charred timbers had survived both
in the post holes and on the floor of the building. The positioning of some of
the timbers suggested there may have been fixed furniture such as benches and
bed boxes. Other features within the floor of the building suggested at least one
loom emplacement within the building, although the dispersed concentration
of loomweights suggests there may have been more.

Only a few fragmented pot sherds were found in and around the structure, but
there was one distinctive piece which displayed a complete section, roughly
decorated with horizontal lines and chevrons. Several large pieces of the vessel

4.7 Bone weaving comb from
Upton weaving shed (length
approx 14cm).

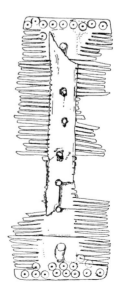

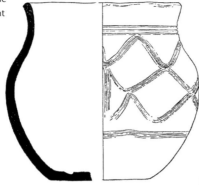

4.8 Beaker-shaped vessel in use when shed burnt down (height approx 14cm).

were found within the burnt daub layer from the collapsed wall. One of these was burnt right through while an adjacent fitting piece with a relatively fresh fracture was buff with little sign of burning. This suggested that the pot was in use when the building caught fire and was broken and scattered by the falling debris so that different pieces suffered different degrees of burning depending on their proximity to the fire. If so, it provided a good date for the destruction of the building of late 6th to early 7th centuries AD.

Twywell Iron Age Settlement

At the end of 1966 another Iron Age site was exposed by quarrying, this time at an ironstone quarry at Twywell near Thrapston, being worked by the South Durham Iron and Steel Company. The site was discovered by Eric Peplow, a member of the local archaeological society, who found a feature containing Iron Age pottery after the topsoil had been stripped. The Society again organised a rescue dig and Dr Dennis Harding and Mr Robertson-Mackay, again visited the site. They were happy with my work at Upton and asked if I would direct the excavation full time.

Again, I had little hesitation accepting – a move which confirmed, or sealed my fate, as a professional archaeologist. This was of course, the middle of the Swinging Sixties when the country was riding a wave of optimism fuelled

4.9 Twywell, 1966 an Iron Age site is exposed as quarrying advances.

by revolutions in fashion, music and sexual behaviour. And there was just as much excitement locally as Northampton Town ('the Cobblers') had risen from the Fourth to the First Division of the Football League in only five years. As Joe Mercer, the ex-England manager famously commented *"The miracle of 1966 was not England winning the World Cup but Northampton Town being in the First Division"*. The only blot on the sporting horizon was the failure by Northamptonshire County Cricket Club to win the County Championship for the first time ever in 1965 when they came second to Worcestershire by a mere 5 points. The title being decided by a rather generous declaration allowing Worcestershire to win on the final day of the season.

Although I was much too old to be part of the flower power generation – and was always more of a Hollies rather than Beatles man anyway – I had supported the Cobblers for many years and may have got caught up in the spirit of the age when I enthusiastically swopped the functional well-heeled bricklayer's trowel for the slighter, more esoteric – and definitely less well-rewarded – trowel of the modern day archaeologist.

This was soon brought home to me when I made more enquiries to the Ministry of Works about pay and expenses in my new career. I was told I could claim a daily fee and travelling expenses but even when combined this was likely to be so low I would probably need to work seven days a week to earn a living wage. This was a big drop in pay compared to what I was earning as a builder and it became quite clear that an archaeological career would be a labour of love.

4.10 1967 Summer of Love, Twywell Quarry, with Stephen, Sandra and Chris probably all wondering what we are doing here.

I subsequently spent most of that year working on the site at Twywell, mostly for seven days a week. Because I was spending so much time away from home I had a caravan on site so that my wife and family could stay at weekends – a very different version of the 1967 Summer of Love on a quarry in Twywell – not quite San Francisco.

The workforce varied over this time from one or two to about twelve depending on requirements and availability. It consisted mainly of students with or without experience and labourers with no experience. Two students who provided valuable assistance throughout the excavation were Terry Panter and Brian Dix from Kettering

Grammar School. They were both members of an archaeological group at the school and had gained experience on excavations carried out by their headmaster John Steane. Another person who worked virtually full time was Jim Pollock, a Scotsman – otherwise known as 'Gideon' – who worked as a singer in the evenings. Despite his lack of experience, Jim Pollock was very reliable and conscientious and was one of the politest men I have ever met – refusing to call me by my Christian name throughout the time he worked on the site.

4.11 And the family joins in; daughter Sandra earns her pocket money at Twywell.

I had the great pleasure in meeting Sir Mortimer Wheeler while working at Twywell, who provided the invaluable advice to *"concentrate on the plan my boy"*. I tried to achieve this by locating and recording every feature as accurately as possible, in the hope that other, more experienced archaeologists, may be able to help with interpretation at a later stage.

By the end of the excavation we had identified four enclosures, two of which had been partly destroyed before the site was discovered. One of the enclosures (Enclosure B) was completely excavated as well as part of a second (Enclosure C). The ditch to both enclosures had been re-dug or cleaned out on numerous occasions, with the deep ditch phase of Enclosure B preceded by a period when the area was enclosed by a succession of palisade fences. Within Enclosure B there were two smaller enclosed compounds, one with a 4-post rectangular structure in the entranceway. The opening faced east with remnants of limestone cobbling, which may have been a trackway leading to Enclosure C.

The number of post holes within Enclosure B suggested that there were structures within the compound, but it is uncertain whether this represented house sites. Alternatively, it is possible that many of the features related to the early palisaded phase, prior to its conversion to a cattle compound. Curving gullies located to the north and west of Enclosure B suggest there may have been as many as eight roundhouses sited in this area; three of which were complete and the remainder indicated by surviving short lengths of gully.

A total of 180 pits were recorded, the majority of which were either completely excavated or sectioned. Roughly half of these were located within Enclosure B, which were the earliest, and the remainder were located to the north of the enclosure ditch. Within the enclosure, seven pits contained articulated burials, three humans (two adults and one child), two dogs and two pigs. One of the adult burials was an adult male whose bones were crushed by large stones either thrown or placed over his body, and the child burial was in a crouched position, with the complete skull of an ox in the same pit. The skeleton of the pig was curled up oddly on a pillow of stones. At that time, we were less aware of the role that religious or ritual activity played in people's lives during the Iron Age and did not recognize that these may have been sacrificial burials.

One pit contained carbonised grain (wheat and barley) which suggested that

4.12 Dog burial in a pit at Twywelll.

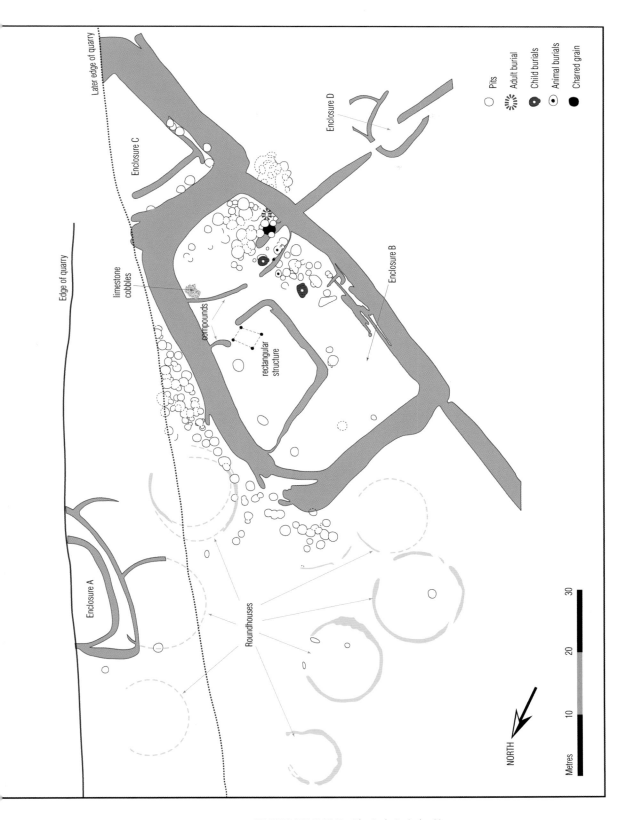

Edge of quarry

Later edge of quarry

Enclosure C

Enclosure D

Enclosure B

limestone cobbles

compounds

rectangular structure

Enclosure A

Roundhouses

NORTH

Metres

10 20 30

Pits

Adult burial

Child burials

Animal burials

Charred grain

4.14 Bone weaving comb from Twywell made from either cow or horse bone (approx height 8cm).

the inhabitants were carrying out arable farming, and there were also a number of clay-lined pits, perhaps used for dyeing wool. The positioning of pits outside the enclosure suggested that the enclosed areas were mainly used for corralling stock. The large number of sheep bones found, together with antler and bone weaving equipment, also suggests that sheep farming played an important role in the economy of the settlement.

A radiocarbon date from carbonised grain in one of the pits was centred on 280 Cal BC[19]. This contributed to the suggested development of the site from a small pallisaded enclosure to a small homestead/village between the 4th and 2nd centuries BC, accompanied by a gradual shift of occupation towards the north through the life of the settlement.

It was clear from the plan – and from the location of the original feature located by Eric Peplow – that the total area of activity was far greater than we were able to record. It was a sobering thought that if the areas to the east and south of the site had been available for examination, many of our conclusions about the development and economy of the settlement may have been revised.

Excavations at that time also differed from today in that there was little attention given to the collection and analysis of environmental data – largely because there was not the facilities or resources now available. It is interesting to consider how the interpretation of the findings – and indeed the direction of the excavation – may have differed with the benefit of this information.

Report Writing in London

When I finished the excavation at Twywell I was asked to go to London to prepare the report. Most of this time was spent in offices in Victoria Street, near Big Ben. This was initially daunting as it was the first report for which I had sole responsibility. My trepidation was probably reflected in an early draft because a Ministry of Works Inspector's response was... *"You must present the reader with a house not a pile of bricks"*. I never knew whether or not he was aware of my building background, but either way, it was a sentiment I would not forget, even though I am still not sure it is correct (acquiring the bricks and having a knowledge of construction is critical, but there are still many different ways in which a house can be built from the same pile of bricks).

While working in London I was fortunate to come into contact with other Ministry of Works' excavators working on reports including Tony Brewster, Ernest Greenfield, Christine Mahoney, Margaret Jones and Stanley West, and the Ministry's scientist Leo Biek. Although none of them seemed particularly interested in what they were doing in London – and much preferred to talk about their next excavations – without realizing it, they all contributed enormously to my understanding of what was required to produce a report to the appropriate standard. It was also fascinating to learn about the major excavations being carried out, such as the site at Mucking being excavated by Margaret Jones, which made me feel involved with developments at the national level.

I would frequently visit the Society of Antiquaries Library in Piccadilly and would often again see the impressive figure of Sir Mortimer Wheeler underneath his big hat. Again, and without realizing it, his mere presence would provide me with inspiration and reassurance that my new career was the right one.

Aldwincle – Neolithic and Bronze Age Burials

While still working at Twywell, I became aware that gravel extraction at Thrapston was being extended to the west of the River Nene into the area of Henslow Meadow in Aldwincle parish. This is the area where I had done much of my original archaeological exploration – and indeed where I had spent much of my childhood – but until that time the two barrows and the Roman Gartree Road were the only features in the archaeological record.

4.15 Barrow in Henslow Meadow 1961 prior to levelling by the farmer.

The barrow sites had been levelled by the farmer in 1963 and the ditches were subsequently revealed by aerial photography. I paid regular visits to the area as the topsoil stripping approached the site of the two former barrow mounds and was able to identify and excavate the large grave pits that were below each mound. Each of the burials was similar, both interred in wooden coffins set in large grave pits with their heads towards the south-south-west. One burial (Barrow 1) was a male, 40–45 years old and almost 6 feet tall. His bones were so well preserved that the bone specialist was able to tell that his nose had been broken and had healed during his lifetime. Lying at his feet were a number of objects including two flint arrowheads, a scraper, a boar's tusk, a rubbing stone and two bone spatulars. The second burial was also a male but the bones were disarticulated. The only object buried with him was a crushed beaker. The grave goods found within the burials dated the site to the Bronze Age Beaker period (around 2000 BC).

4.16 Burial in Barrow 1, found in a boat shaped coffin with grave goods at his feet.

It was a strange experience to excavate an area I had known so well and played on as a child and to realize that the site had been used for human burial so long ago. Strangely, as a child during the war, I saw two planes collide in mid-air and found the wreckage of the aircraft and the dead crew in Henslow Meadow not far from the burial sites. I frequently found bits of metal when working on and around the prehistoric burials which provoked rather eerie feeling about the nature of time and human mortality (definitely echoes of John Clare).

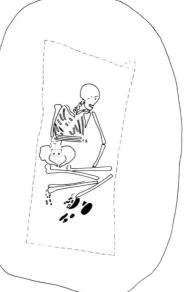

This excavation was not easy because the gravel company would not give us permission to get to the site via their access road. Instead, each of our

4.17 Aldwincle, Neolithic mortuary enclosure, an articulated burial, foreground, and a disarticulated burial found between two large post holes (one shown at top of picture).

visits was down a rough track from Islip village. The quarry manager, Dougy Peck, did not want us on the site and gave us little co-operation. Fortunately, the digger driver, Ray Crute, was prepared to help us as much as he could providing his manager did not see him.

The topsoil stripping also revealed a Neolithic mortuary enclosure aligned with the two barrows, some 75 metres to the west. When first revealed, roughly half of the feature had been scraped down to gravel level with a subsequent loss of evidence. We were fortunate in being able to excavate much of the other half from the ground surface. Luckily, evidence for a mortuary structure survived with two burials, one articulated in a tightly crouched position and the other deposited as a heap of disarticulated bone, lying between two large post holes. The burials lay directly on the old surface and had the topsoil clearance extended a further metre to the north all evidence would have been lost.

The large post holes at either end of the burials had supported massive posts at least 70cm in width, which were probably the end posts of a timber mortuary house. A second pair of post pits were found in a central position within the monument but any trace of burials had been removed by medieval ridge and furrow cultivation.

The site had a number of phases of development, with the earliest period producing an uncalibrated radiocarbon date centred on 2600bc[20] which, in 1968, was the earliest recorded site in the county. The final phase was likely to have been the digging of an outer ditch to create a barrow or mound over the mortuary enclosure. A ditch dug in the early Roman period curved around this area, presumably to avoid a mound, but the centre was later truncated by ridge and furrow cultivation, which suggests that the mound was levelled either before or during the medieval period. The site of the enclosure is now beneath a large lake, but a short length of the outer ditch presumably survives beneath an electricity pylon, which still provides a useful marker of the site's location.

My helpers on this site were largely inexperienced and I left plenty of baulks to try to understand the complex stratigraphy. By then relations with the gravel company had improved and when the directors visited the site they thought the baulks were walls and were amazed at how I knew they were there. There were some eccentric people working on the site, including a retired building labourer,

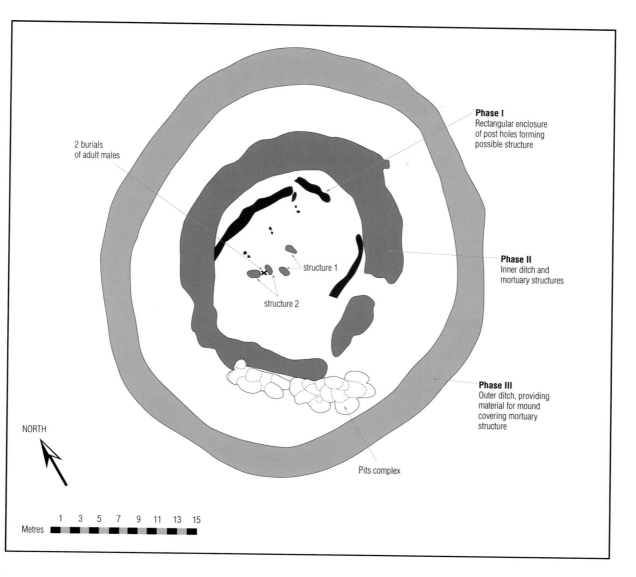

Phase I
Rectangular enclosure
of post holes forming
possible structure

2 burials
of adult males

structure 1

structure 2

Phase II
Inner ditch and
mortuary structures

Phase III
Outer ditch, providing
material for mound
covering mortuary
structure

Pits complex

NORTH

Metres
1 3 5 7 9 11 13 15

4.18 Plan of Neolithic mortuary
enclosure at Aldwincle.

George Wilson, who provided valuable assistance and a soft-hearted teenager, Robin Goodfellow, who would frequently take birds that had been injured flying into the overhead cables, the 10 miles into Kettering for treatment.

As further topsoil was stripped it became clear just how rich the area was in archaeological remains. My work at Twywell was now drawing to a close so I concentrated all my efforts on recovering the archaeological data being rapidly destroyed by the quarrying at Aldwincle. The further finds that we made in the area fully justified this decision.

This included two ring ditches which were excavated just to the west of the mortuary enclosure. These were also of Neolithic date and may have been broadly contemporary with the mortuary enclosure. One had a continuous ditch enclosing a platform of 30m diameter and a possible empty grave in the centre; the second enclosed a platform of 25 metres and had a pit dug into the ditch containing a human skull sealed between two slabs of stone.

Just to the south-west of the Neolithic enclosure, we found the remains of 11 cremations at gravel level after a considerable depth of overburden had been removed. These were unurned, but associated pottery suggested they were no later than Bronze Age. Most of the cremation pits had been scraped away and it seems likely that there were others that had not survived. Parts of two Bronze Age urns were also found in the vicinity which supports a date of this period for the cremations.

Aldwincle Iron Age Settlement

In 1969, part of an Iron Age enclosure was partially exposed by the quarrying to the west of the earlier features. This was excavated at the time, and we returned in 1971 to excavate the remaining area when plans were revealed to divert a stream through the site. My labour force on this site consisted of one person with experience, Brian Dix, who had worked at Twywell, and labourers that were recruited from Northampton Labour Exchange. Some of these clearly did not want to work and were constantly seeking a reason to be sacked. They refused to use a brush or small tools – presumably because it challenged their macho personas – and one of them deliberately stepped into a post hole full of water before marching off site saying *"Well I can't work now"*.

The enclosure was roughly rectangular in shape, not dissimilar, but larger than the earlier site at Twywell. The enclosure ditch had been recut on at least one occasion and had an entrance on the southern side during the second phase of use. This had an inset timber gateway flanked on either side by a length of stone wall or stockade.

The enclosure contained four roundhouses, of which only three could have stood at the same time. On the basis of the pottery evidence, Hut 2 was the earliest, and the most soundly constructed building and

4.19 Hut 2, wall trench during excavation.

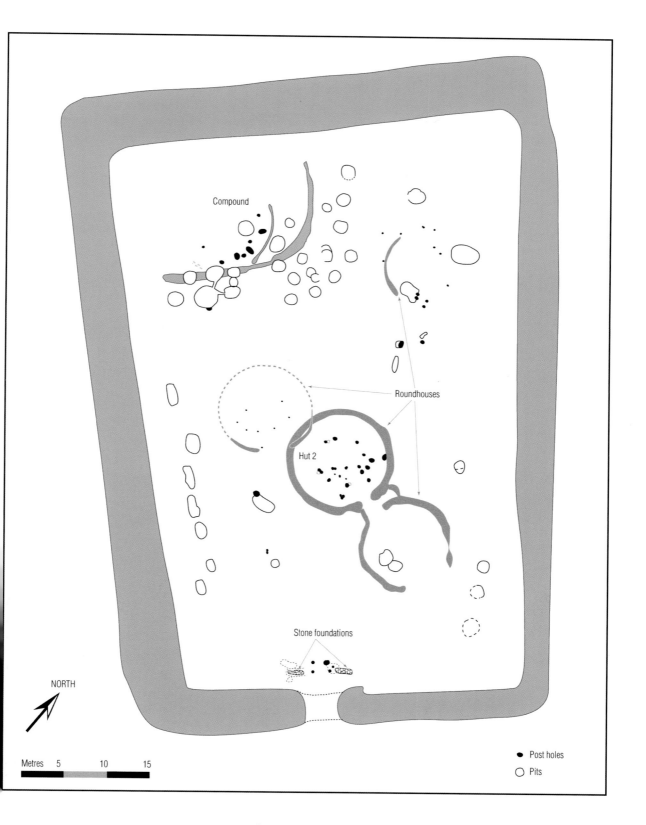

Compound

Roundhouses

Hut 2

Stone foundations

NORTH

Metres 5 10 15

● Post holes
○ Pits

PREVIOUS PAGE
4.20 Plan of Iron Age settlement
at Aldwincle.

may have stood alone during the earliest phase. The house wall was formed by a ring of split timbers (an estimated 124 in total) placed in a bedding trench and probably interwoven with wattles. Immediately outside of this was a second line of around 24 posts set a maximum of 2 metres apart. These would have supported a similar number of roof rafters, supported by a ring beam morticed to an inner ring of posts within the hut itself. Ten inner post holes were recorded, but as the hut had at least two phases, the number in use at any one time may have been as few as four or five.

In the western corner of the settlement there was a small internal enclosure which may have been used as an animal pen, and a group of 24 pits. The limited number of pits may indicate that the inhabitants had limited storage requirements – perhaps because of a reliance on animal husbandry rather than cereal production – or that the site was not in use for a very long period of time.

4.21 Betty keeps the hut clean while son Chris is more interested in the photographer.

The pottery recovered from the excavated features dated the site to the late 2nd-early 1st century BC.

I moved the caravan to the site and my family would again visit for weekends. The area had been left uncultivated and we had to make a path through head-high weeds to get to the van. It was a very peaceful and atmospheric site, especially when wandering through the excavations in the moonlight and experiencing the strong sense of place inhabited by our prehistoric forebears.

Aldwincle Roman Bridge

We were aware that a Roman Road (the Gartree Road from Leicester to Godmanchester) ran adjacent to a hedgerow on the north-east side of Henslow Meadow. After the overburden had been stripped from the line of the road there appeared to be a high ridge of natural gravel denoting its route. We later realized that this was the result of Roman quarrying for gravel on either side of the road.

One evening I was wandering along the course of the road when I noticed massive timbers revealed in the quarry face highlighted by the dying rays of the setting sun. This was part of the abutment of a Roman bridge surviving *in situ* that carried the road across a buried watercourse, presumably the River Nene. In hindsight, we were very fortunate that the side of the bridge was revealed in the quarry face just a few days before it would have been totally destroyed without record.

Once again we had a problem with the quarry manager who insisted that the structure was modern and that he needed to quarry the area the following week. Fuelled by a mixture of excitement and panic, I contacted the County Architect John Goff who immediately agreed to visit the site and he, in turn, invited the directors of the company to visit. They were very interested and said I could have as much time as I needed to excavate the bridge. I was relieved but knew it wouldn't do much to improve relations with the quarry manager.

Excavation of the bridge showed it to have three main structural periods, indicated by the three adjacent rows of vertical piles located near the abutment and by three distinct layers of road-metalling visible in the silted up river bed. Lying on the old river bed were a number of collapsed timbers which would have originally formed part of the bridge during the first period. Pottery found with these timbers suggested that the bridge first collapsed no earlier than just after the end of the first century AD. The bridge was reconstructed and pottery suggests it remained in use throughout the Hadriannic and Antonine periods[21] The bridge collapsed again, possibly around the beginning of the 3rd century AD. Rebuilt once more, the horizontal timbers found in position had formed part of the bridge abutment of this final phase. There was no evidence for the date of the final collapse but again is likely to have been sometime during the 3rd century AD.

The surviving timbers were solid oak, and the largest were up to 7 metres long by 0.5 metres square with deep mortices cut into them. We were helped enormously by the skill of the digger driver, Eddie from Barton Seagrave. He managed to remove the silt and clay from around the timbers by machine without damaging them and then successfully dragged them out with a rope. The wood was very heavy and after it had been loaded onto a lorry, the vehicle sank up to its axles in the soft ground. It was amusing to see the lorry being dragged across the field by a bulldozer like a sledge, as the quarry manager looked on in horror as his access road was churned up.

There were four human burials found near the approaches to the bridge, one of which was a skeleton lying on its side with a small iron knife protruding from its ribs. Thoughts of murder and mayhem on the bridge were confounded by the fact that the knife was dated to the 7th century. The other burials could not be dated but it is feasible that there was a small Saxon cemetery situated in the vicinity, perhaps associated with a nearby water hole (see later).

For such an important site it was pity that I only had one helper available at the time, Graham Clayson from Bozeat. It was also mid winter and as there was no shelter on the site, the combination of wintery conditions and a wintery relationship with the quarry manager, did not make for a very a pleasant working environment. But we were of course fortified by the exciting nature of the excavation. Unfortunately, there was a foot and mouth outbreak at the time and the quarry manager did his best to prevent visitors, including, sadly, members of the local history society from visiting the site.

The Ministry of Works had asked us to remove and save as many timbers as possible. The wood was wrapped in black polythene and stored in an open shed at Kirby Hall. This proved to be unsatisfactory and the wood soon started to deteriorate; as far as I know none of it remains today. Conversely, a piece of wood I stored in my cellar dried out over a period of time and is still in good condition today. It was a pity that it was not possible to preserve the bridge *in situ* especially as there was so little commercial gravel below the stream bed.

Quarrying continued to the north-east of Henslow Meadow into the 1970s. We excavated a number of features in the area, but as we were not working full time at the quarry there may have been others destroyed without record. This included an Anglo-Saxon water hole, consisting of a wattle and daub timber structure set in a large pit. The timberwork was composed of thin branches of ash, hazel and blackthorn interwoven around vertical stakes of oak, alder and hazel. The

4.24 The Anglo-Saxon water hole excavated at Aldwincle.

4.25 Pit alignment at Aldwincle shown to be earlier than the Roman road.

stakes had been roughly shaped and driven into the gravel. The north side of the water-hole had been filled with layers of stone set between horizontal planks, presumably to form steps to provide access to the water hole. A single radiocarbon date from wattles in the structure gave an uncalibrated date range of 700-840ad[22].

Further excavations included a pit alignment which was traced for a distance of almost 300 metres and contained over 40 pits. Like similar features elsewhere, there was little evidence of function or date. It was clearly earlier than the Roman road it intersected which was supported by the fill which suggested an early Iron Age date. There was evidence of a considerable degree of care in their construction with pits displaying regular spacing, shape and depth. The alignment ran almost parallel with Harpers Brook to the east and may have formed an intersection with an undated ditch to the south which ran at right angles to the alignment. This may represent a similar arrangement to that discovered later at Grendon (see following chapters).

Henslow Meadow is now underwater and is an attractive environment for walkers, anglers and bird-watchers. Few visitors will be aware of the wealth of archaeological features discovered in the area. Only the line of electricity pylons remain as markers to position the various sites that were excavated within this lost landscape. These sites are only in the archaeological record because we were fortunate enough to be in the right place at the right time and had the resources (as limited as they were) and enthusiasm (as unlimited as it was) to ensure that they were recovered before being lost for all time.

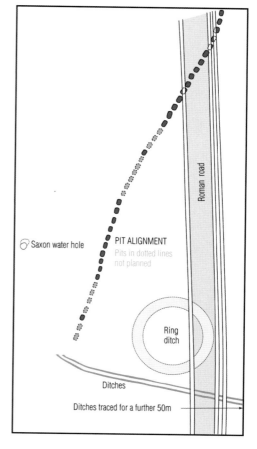

Saxon water hole

PIT ALIGNMENT
Pits in dotted lines not planned

Roman road

Ring ditch

Ditches

Ditches traced for a further 50m

4.26 Plan showing all sites at Henslow Meadow, Aldwincle. (Green arrow shows position and direction of image shown in 4.27 below).

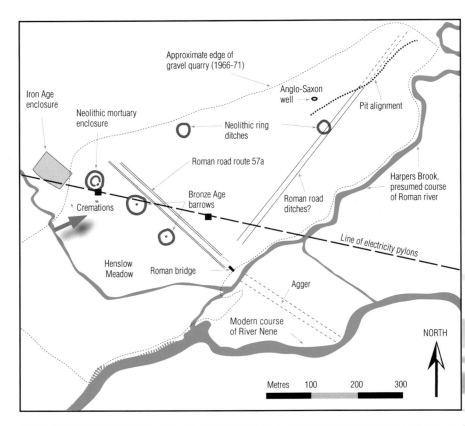

Approximate edge of gravel quarry (1966-71)

Iron Age enclosure

Neolithic mortuary enclosure

Anglo-Saxon well

Pit alignment

Neolithic ring ditches

Roman road route 57a

Harpers Brook, presumed course of Roman river

Cremations

Bronze Age barrows

Roman road ditches?

Line of electricity pylons

Henslow Meadow

Roman bridge

Agger

Modern course of River Nene

NORTH

Metres 100 200 300

4.27 2009 view across line of electricity pylons. (see 4.26 above).

Earls Barton Barrow

The next threat from gravel quarrying, brought to my attention by Dick Hollowell, was a previously unrecorded bell barrow at Earls Barton clearly visible in the floodplan of the River Nene from the now disused railway line from Northampton to Peterborough. Due to the imminent quarrying we had to excavate the site in the winter time during the early months of 1969 and I was fortunate in receiving urgent assistance from John Pallistor and other workers from Tony Brewster's excavations in Yorkshire. They were experienced in excavating barrows and we adopted their methods of using wide trenches rather than the traditional quadrant system. This provided plenty of sections and these proved invaluable in helping to understand a mound badly disturbed by animals burrowing into the light loam soil.

4.28 Plan of Earls Barton barrow.

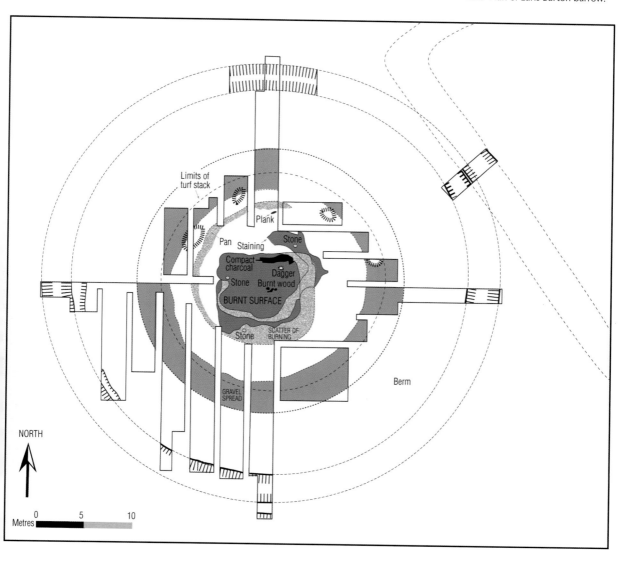

Limits of
turf stack

Plank

Pan Staining   Stone

Compact
charcoal   Dagger
Stone   Burnt wood

BURNT SURFACE

Stone   SCATTER OF
BURNING

Berm

GRAVEL
SPREAD

NORTH

0   5   10
Metres

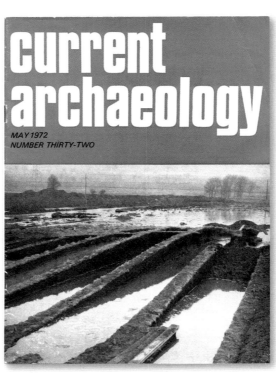

4.29 Cover of Current Archaeology, May 1972, showing Earls Barton barrow under water.

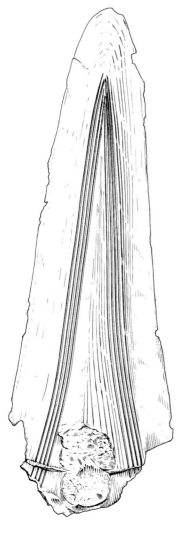

4.30 The bronze ogival dagger found at Earls Barton (approx height 18cm).

current archaeology

MAY 1972
NUMBER THIRTY-TWO

Unfortunately the site had to be abandoned part of the way through due to snow and then floods. This made a mess of our baulks but provided some spectacular photographs one of which found its way onto the front cover of an early edition of *Current Archeology* (No 32).

The only finds of note were a scatter of cremated bones in association with a ogival dagger of the Bronze Age Wessex type found just north-east of the centre of the barrow. The bones amounted to only 8g in weight but their proximity to the dagger suggested an interment disturbed by animal burrows. Radiocarbon dates taken from wood and charcoal lying on the pre-barrow surface proved to be extremely controversial. Two dates, both apparently in the 13th century BC (1264 and 1219bc) were the first for the Bronze Age Wessex Culture and were later than some academics expected (or wanted). As a result, I was summoned to a heated meeting at the Society of Antiquaries to discuss these findings. On the one side was Professor Renfrew who argued that the Wessex Culture was earlier in date, and on the other was Professor Hawkes who was happy with the new date. Perhaps not surprisingly the argument descended to a discussion of my credentials – especially my background and academic ability – for providing such information. Despite Professor Hawkes describing me as *'one of the best rural excavators in the country'*, Professor Renfrew insisted that the date could not be right, finally shouting across the room that I represented *'the first swallow in a very long summer'*.

Subsequently, with the recognition that radiocarbon dates did not directly correspond to calendar years, and the consequent need to calibrate dates, the Earls Barton date became more acceptable to (most) of the wider archaeological community. The dates can now be seen to place the Earls Barton barrow towards the end of the early Bronze Age, at around 1500–1400 BC[23].

This was the only time when I regretted not having a formal archaeological degree level qualification. It made me realize that for some people this provided more credibility than any amount of practical knowledge and experience gained over the years in the field.

Wakerley – Anglo-Saxon Cemetery

Towards the end of the 1960s I spent a lot of time working on the ironstone quarries operated by British Steel to the north of Kettering, particularly along the escarpment of the River Welland between Corby and Stamford. When the topsoil was stripped from a new quarry on a hillside at Wakerley, I walked the area and discovered many human bones spread across the windswept site. I soon realized we had a newly exposed Saxon cemetery and that as very little had been destroyed we had the rare opportunity of excavating a complete cemetery site.

Locating the graves was difficult because they had been backfilled with the same subsoil through which they were excavated. Often the alignment of small stones in the backfill was the only indication of disturbance. Once I realized this I became quite adept at locating burials, teasing my fellow workers by appearing to use my shovel as a dowser. The first burial we excavated created local interest and some grave goods disappeared on the first night; thereafter we had to start and finish the excavation of a grave in a day or make sure that the location of grave goods was not obvious.

The first phase of the excavation was carried out in the winter of 1968/69 when the combination of exposed site, north-easterly wind and frozen ground made it a cold and bleak place to work, especially when excavating skeletons did little to raise the body temperature. I was helped by Terry Panter and Jon Small from Northampton, whose raconteur story telling made the long journey from the town each day more bearable. Jon was determined to provide protection from the elements and built himself a tent using the metal poles he used for a lightshow in the evenings, only to return the next day to find a heap of twisted metal in the nearest hedgerow.

The second stage, carried out in the summer of 1970, was a much more pleasant affair. At the end of the excavation I was confident that all the graves had been found, although some may have been ploughed away before 1968. I examined the blank areas mechanically to ensure we had not missed any.

Overall, a total of 85 burials were found in 72 graves. It would seem that the cemetery was laid out within a fairly short space of time, although a single period event such as a plague, was rejected in favour of a 6th-early 7th century date range, covering more than one generation. All the graves were roughly cut with rounded corners, but the multiple burial graves tended to be more evenly cut with more angular corners, suggesting that the grave was planned to take more than one burial from the outset (which, perversely, could support the plague hypothesis).

4.31 Cruciform brooch from Wakerley (Leeds florid type) found in female grave (approx height 17cm).

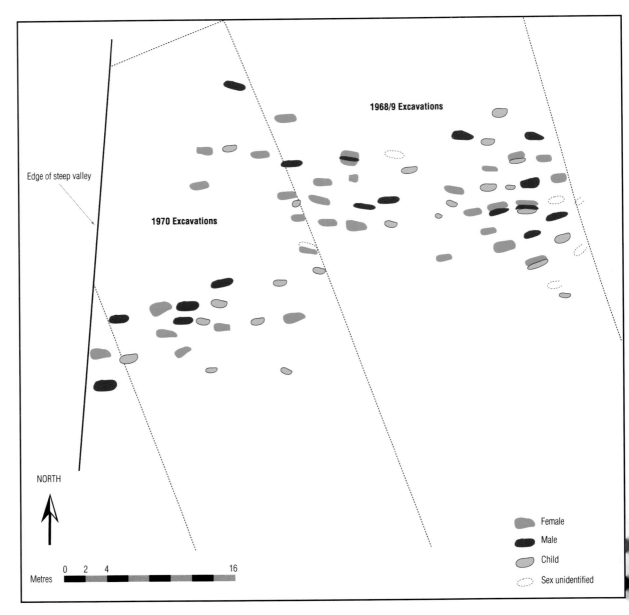

1968/9 Excavations

Edge of steep valley

1970 Excavations

NORTH

Female
Male
Child
Sex unidentified

0 2 4   16
Metres

4.32 Plan of Anglo-Saxon
cemetery at Wakeley.

Many of the bones did not survive and those that did were in relatively poor condition. Nevertheless analysis of the surviving bone suggested that all the individuals were aged between one and forty-five, with the majority being female (65%). Almost all the burials were aligned roughly east-west with heads at the west end. The men tended to be laid out straight with arms at the side of the body or with the left arm only across the body. Women were often found in a flexed position with crossed legs and the head placed to the left.

In an exception to this pattern, a man was buried face downwards with his head to the east and his arms and legs in such a position to suggest that he had been bound before burial. One can only speculate on the reasoning behind such a

4.33 A double burial at Wakerley.

ABOVE
4.34 Bronze pins from a female grave (approx length 11cm).

BELOW
4.35 Tinned bronze buckle from a juvenile grave (approx length 2.5cm).

dramatic departure from normal practice, but given the religious significance of burial practice for the pagan Anglo-Saxons, it can only be presumed the man had seriously transgressed accepted social behaviour within the group.

Over 400 grave goods were found with the burials. These were a mixture of cheap items such as small-long brooches or swastika brooches, with good quality square headed and florid cruciforms. Unusual items included a drinking horn; a lozenze shaped mount, perhaps from a harness set; a complete example of a florid cruciform brooch of Leeds type and a runic inscription scratched on a square-headed brooch. There were also a number of so-called buckets (about the size of a paint tin). These had been made with very thin strips of wood (like plywood) and it was surprising to find the wood so well preserved by the salts from the bronze strips binding the buckets. There were so many objects

4.36 Silver hook and eye wrist clasps from a female grave.

recovered that our small hut frequently looked like a treasure trove with bronze brooches and amulets competing with more mundane cups and utensils for drying space.

4.37 Square-headed brooch with runic inscription ('*Buhu*') on reverse (left front, right rear from a female grave (approx height 11cm).

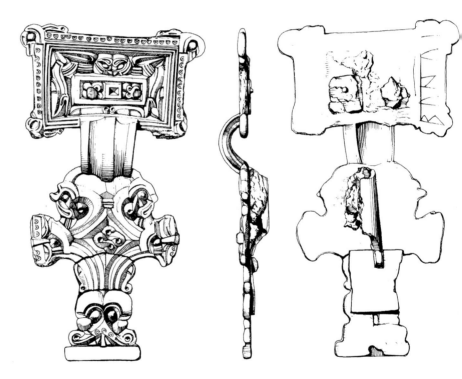

Weekley Hall Wood and Other Excavations

A number of other smaller excavations were also carried out during this period, all on sites threatened by quarrying, including an early Iron Age settlement at Weekley Hall Wood. Evidence of early prehistoric settlements do not survive well and is often difficult to locate by ground or aerial survey. Brian Dix and myself spent many weeks clearing a area of bedrock by hand and although only a few sherds of pottery were recovered the eventual plan contained 96 post

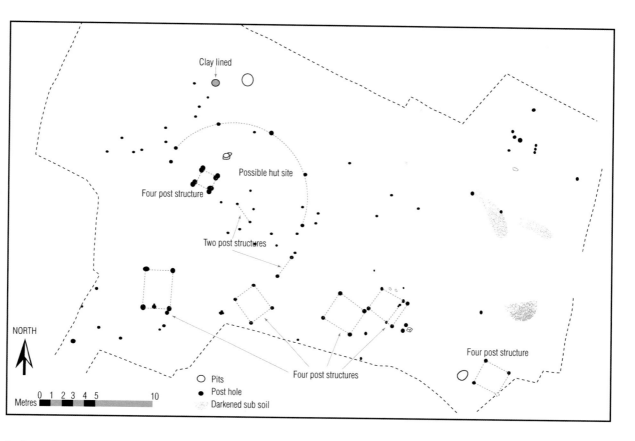

Figure labels (as shown on plan):
Clay lined
Possible hut site
Four post structure
Two post structures
NORTH
Four post structures
Four post structure
Pits
Post hole
Darkened sub soil
0 1 2 3 4 5   10
Metres

holes reflecting at least six four-post structures and a possible house site. This demonstrated the difficulty of locating sites of the late Bronze-early Iron Age where there are few if any pits or ditches. The site was adjacent to a ditched trackway of presumably the same date.

Another difficult excavation was carried out on a pit alignment at Briar Hill Farm, Northampton where we were working in house foundations and amongst stacks of bricks. This revealed a unique plan of a row of square pits replacing a line of smaller circular pits, probably post holes. Numerous small scraps of pottery were found in the pits dating to the later Bronze Age-early Iron Age period. Interestingly, the alignment heads towards the roundabout in Rothersthorpe Road and is presumably preserved underneath this.

Back on the ironstone quarries, much of what had been Rockingham Forest was cut down during the Second World War to make way for quarrying. In both Bulwick and Gretton parishes, the remains of iron smelting furnaces and associated channel hearths were revealed by soil stripping prior to quarrying. In 1969, the ironstone deposit at Brookfield Quarry at Bulwick was being quarried at a depth of 30 metres, but the early furnace workers were smelting the ironstone nodules and using the Estuarine clay to build the structures, both of which were obtainable on or near the surface. On typological grounds the furnaces are thought to date to the Roman period.

4.38 Plan of Early Iron Age settlement at Weekley Hall Wood.

Towards the End of the Decade

The experience gained during these early years left me with a much better understanding of the extent to which archaeological sites – and indeed whole landscapes – in the county were being destroyed by development, especially quarrying for ironstone and gravel extraction. This had of course to become a topic of urgent national debate following the publication of *A Matter of Time*[24] in 1960 which drew attention to the large scale destruction of archaeological sites by gravel quarrying. By now I also had a good understanding of the sacrifices that were required to pursue a career in archaeology, or at least the hours that had to be worked to earn a basic wage. But the knowledge that there was so little else being done to rescue and record sites prior to destruction provided a massive stimulus to continue with this work, irrespective of any personal consequences.

Also at this time, a number of Development Corporations were being set up in the area to oversee the expansion of towns such as Northampton, Peterborough and Milton Keynes. It was obvious that many archaeological sites were going to be destroyed by these developments and I contacted the Chief Architect for Northampton, Gordon Redfern, to see if he was aware of this. He was not, and immediately arranged a meeting with various interested parties, including Mr Robertson-Mackay from the Ministry of Works, to discuss what should be done. It was agreed that Northampton Development Corporation would appoint an archaeology officer to oversee development in and around the town. I was asked if I wanted the job but declined as I was so heavily involved in rescue work on the quarries, and knew that if I did not do this no-one else would. The job was subsequently offered to Dennis Mynard, and although he, and his successor John Williams, both ended up being much better off financially than I was, I never regretted this decision. It meant that I was free to continue my rescue work on the Northamptonshire quarries during the coming decade.

CHAPTER FIVE

1970s: The Middle Period

"The best way to avoid a bad action is by doing a good one,
for there is no difficulty in the world like that of trying to do nothing"

John Clare

Almost all of my time in the 1970s was spent excavating Iron Age and Roman sites on the gravel and ironstone quarries in the county. This included major excavations on the ironstone quarries in the north of the county at Wakerley and Weekley, and other sites in the Welland valley area including Harringworth and Gretton, and also sites in the Corby and Geddington areas. Work was also carried out on the gravel quarries in the Nene Valley, including sites at Grendon and Ringstead. Finally, towards the end of the decade – and as a precursor of things to come – work was carried out on non-quarry sites at Brigstock and Oundle. Of the many sites I investigated over this time, around 90% were Iron Age or originated in this period. By the end of this time, I felt I had acquired considerable expertise in the identification, excavation and interpretation of Iron Age sites.

Wakerley

The Anglo-Saxon cemetery site that we excavated at Wakerley was situated on the south-east edge of a deep cleft cutting through the hillside at right angles to the Welland valley – somewhat spookily known locally as Dead Man's Hollow. By 1972, quarrying had reached the north-west side of the cleft and had exposed the site of a large Iron Age and Romano-British agricultural and industrial settlement. The site was subsequently excavated at intermittent periods between 1972 and 1975.

The scale of the excavations required a much larger workforce than I was used to on previous sites. I was fortunate in having the support of Pat Foster, who provided much valuable assistance on the site and also drew all the Iron Age pottery; Peter Woods, who excavated all the Roman kilns, and Roy Turland, who described and illustrated all the Roman pottery. I also employed a number of students from Northampton Grammar School, enlisted by my son Stephen.

Iron Age activity at the site extended over three distinct phases. The earliest period, dated to the 3rd century BC, consisted of a stockade and lengths of discontinuous ditch which ran parallel to the top edge of the cleft. The ditches may have been quarries for a bank, and both they and the stockade could have been designed as a defensive feature.

OVERLEAF
5.1 Plan of Wakerley Iron Age settlement.
5.2 Plan of Wakerley Roman settlement.

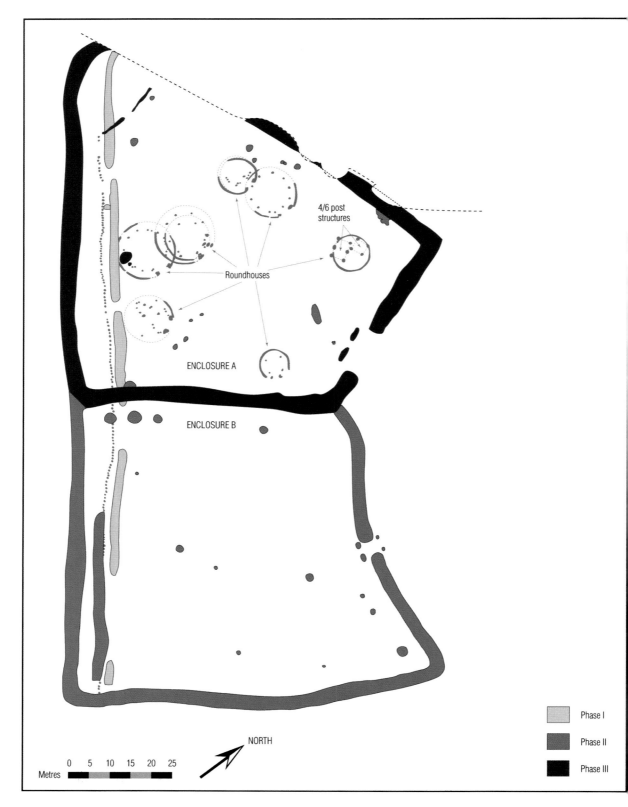

4/6 post structures

Roundhouses

ENCLOSURE A

ENCLOSURE B

NORTH

Metres

0   5   10   15   20   25

Phase I

Phase II

Phase III

ENCLOSURE A

ENCLOSURE B

Aisled barn

NORTH

Metres
0 5 10 15 20 25

■ Roman features
including corn
drying/pottery kilns

■ Early Roman

⬭ Anglo Saxon burials

⬭ Burials of an uncertain date

5.3 View showing Ditch B in the foreground and the position of the settlement in the Welland Valley.

5.4 Reconstruction of statuette of Minerva based on five fragments found at Wakerley (approx height 21cm) .

During the second phase, dated to the 2nd century BC, a squarish area at the south-east end of the site was enclosed by a ditch, thought to be used as a stock compound (Enclosure B). There were seven circular huts to the north-west of the enclosure, although a number of these either overlapped or were reconstructed, suggesting a maximum of five in use at any one time. Although the huts varied in size, they displayed a marked uniformity in design. They all had outer walls constructed with vertical posts and wattle work and an inner ring of posts carrying a ring beam to support the roof. Perhaps surprisingly, with plenty of local limestone available, there was no evidence that stone was used in the construction of the huts. There was also no evidence that the huts were enclosed during this second phase.

The third phase, in the 1st century AD, saw the ditch to Enclosure B filled and a new trapezoidal enclosure, (Enclosure A), was constructed to the north-west. This included a small separate animal pen, which suggests the enclosure was built to enclose the settlement area rather than to coral stock. There was also a succession of 4-post and 6-post structures located on the west side of the enclosure, in what was possibly the best position to have a lookout tower overlooking the Welland valley. The final 6-post structure appears to have been either replaced by a circular structure or was encased within it. There was little evidence to suggest that occupation of the huts inside the enclosure continued into the Roman period.

There were only 26 pits, mostly small, found within either of the two enclosures which may either indicate a modest population or a largely pastoral economy, or it may simply reflect the later date of the site when the use of storage pits was less common. In addition to the normal subsistence economy, there was clear evidence from iron slag deposits found across the site that iron working was being carried out during this period.

During the Roman period, the ditch to Enclosure A silted up, and activity was concentrated in the area previously occupied by Enclosure B and land to the north-east of this, which was enclosed by a series of new ditches. Ceramic evidence suggests that this new enclosure was created by the end of the first century AD and continued to at least the end of the 3rd century.

A Roman timber aisled barn was situated on the south-east side of the enclosed area. This consisted of two rows of eight large post holes for the roof supports and an outer post trench or gully which would have held an external wall. It was estimated that the barn would have been about 20 metres long by 11 metres wide, and is dated to sometime between the mid-second and mid-third centuries.

5.5 Sunken shaft furnace at Wakerley.

Just to the north of the barn were three Romano-British pottery kilns, each with a conventional updraught and subterranean furnace, flue and stoke-hole. In addition, there were a further 47 Roman kilns, ovens or hearths found on the site, some of which included charred grain suggesting they were used as corn-drying kilns. Further evidence of industrial activity on the site was provided by the widespread distribution of features connected with iron working, especially a concentration of 20 iron smelting furnaces and associated features both within and to the south of Enclosure B.

5.6 How many people does it take to remove a sunken shaft furnace?

These included a number of unusual, if not unique, sunken shaft furnaces in which the shaft was built in a pit with no provision for tapping the slag. Dating evidence for these furnaces was sparse but they are likely to date to between the 1st century BC and 1st century AD. Two of these furnaces were lifted and taken to the Natural History Museum in London.

There were 19 inhumation burials found in various locations across the site. Of these, four were Roman; seven others may have been Roman but could not be accurately dated, and eight appeared to form part of a small Anglo-Saxon cemetery. In addition, there were 14 infant burials found, none of which could be dated any later than the 1st century AD.

There was little evidence of habitation during the Roman period and there were very few animal bones found within features of this period. As well as suggesting a switch away from pastoral towards arable farming, this also tends to

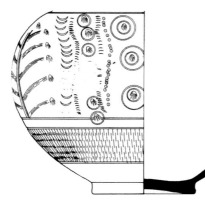

confirm that the site was not in domestic use but was predominantly an agricultural and industrial area. A sort of early industrial estate where people worked during the day but retired to their homes in more salubrious locations away from the often bleak and exposed north-facing ridge.

And, like most industrial estates, it also had its share of failed enterprises. It was clear that pottery production at Wakerley was a short lived and not all together successful venture with less than a dozen sherds found on the site (other than in the kilns themselves). At no time were pots from the kilns ever in use, either at Wakerley or any other site, which seems to have been due entirely to the inexperience of the local potters, as the local Estuarine Series clays are perfectly suitable for pottery making. Perhaps an early example of how failure to invest in staff recruitment and training can jeopardize the best of intentions.

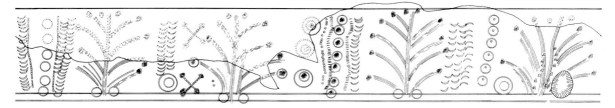

ABOVE
5.8 Detail from jar above showing rivet plug repair (bottom corner, far right). Only high status pottery was usually repaired.

RIGHT
5.9 Photography at Wakerley in the days before Health and Safety legislation.

Gretton/Harringworth

At the same time that this work was being carried out, we also discovered the site of a Roman building in Harringworth parish just 600 metres to the south of the Wakerley site. The site was identified by the pottery scatter and we were, unusually, able to excavate from the surface before quarrying reached the area. The foundations were very shallow but despite this some stonework survived in the foundation trenches and an area of pitched-stone flooring was found in the internal area.

The building had two phases; the first being at least 26 metres long by 9 metres wide, with an internal division creating a smaller area approximately 10 metres square. The south wall was traced for a further 14 metres to the west suggesting that it may have formed part of a larger structure. During the second phase, this was replaced by a larger building, 28 metres by 12 metres, with internal walls at the west end and two post pads for roof support on the north side. A small amount of painted wall plaster was recovered from the building which suggests it also had a domestic use.

The building was excavated in the summer time and with no quarrying in the immediate area it was a peaceful spot which was a blaze of colour with poppies everywhere. I again brought the caravan to the site and my wife and family were able to stay at weekends. There were times like this – especially when wandering over the site in the evening time – when, despite the long hours and poor remuneration, it was hard to imagine a better or more satisfying existence.

At Park Lodge quarry in the adjacent parish of Gretton, we discovered a number of Iron Age boundaries and trackways, dating from the 8th to 4th centuries. We uncovered 40 pits in an alignment and excavated nine of them. They were particularly well preserved as they were dug into limestone and the steep-sided slopes were less prone to erosion but also because they appeared to have been deliberately back filled.

Pit alignments are a common feature of the prehistoric landscape with over 140 examples now known in Northamptonshire alone. Despite their ubiquitous nature, the exact purpose of pit alignments remains uncertain, largely because of their precise spacing, size and shape. At Gretton there was hardly any variation in the spacing of the pits from centre to centre. They were all semi-rectangular or square (like an inverted, truncated pyramid) and dug to a depth of between 70cm and one metre into the bedrock. This profile would not have been easy to achieve with primitive tools and it would have been easier to dig a traditional ditch if the purpose was to create a boundary with a bank.

5.10 Excavated pit alignments at Gretton showing rectangular shape and square bottom.

FOLLOWING PAGE
5.11 Plan of Roman building at Harringworth.

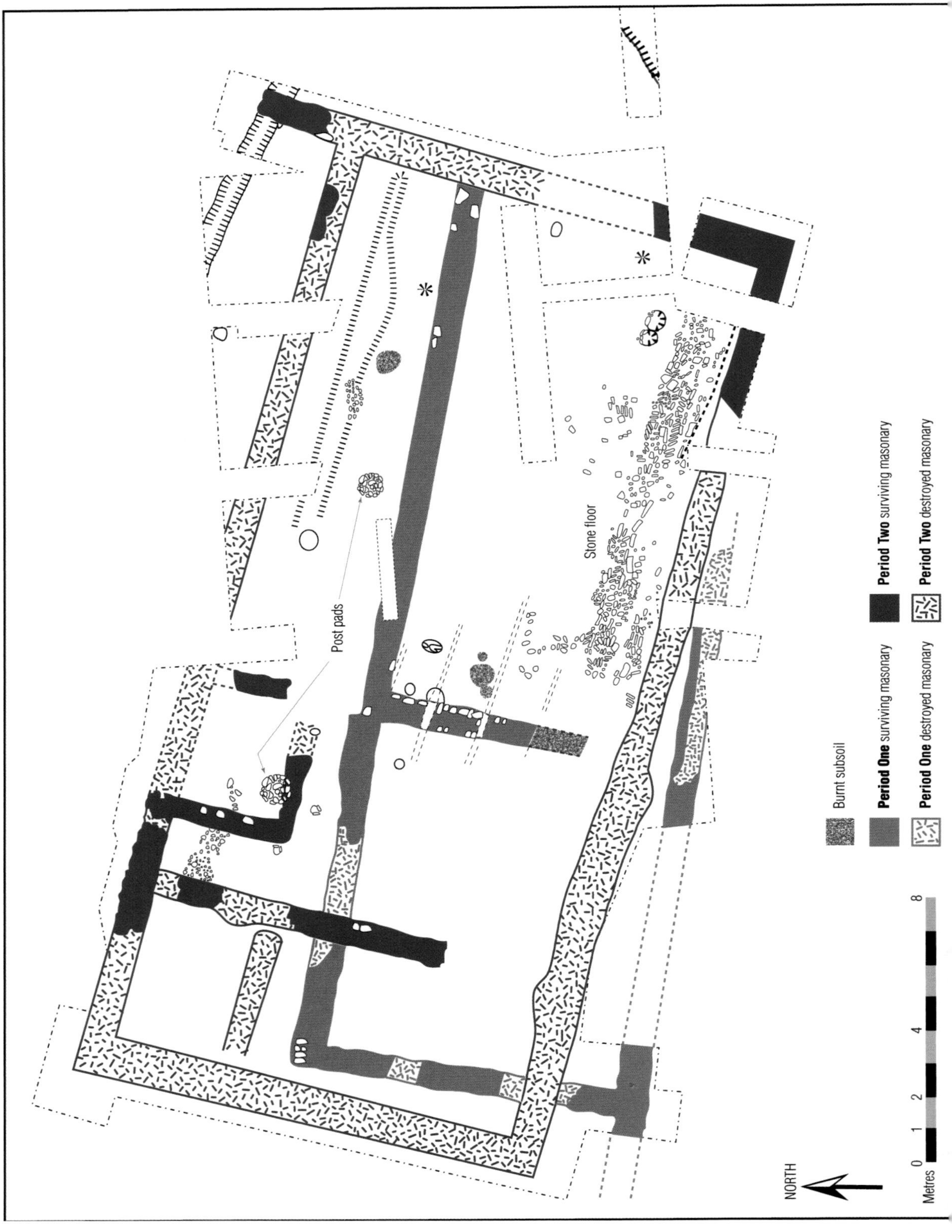

Stone floor

Post pads

Burnt subsoil

Period One surviving masonary

Period One destroyed masonary

Period Two surviving masonary

Period Two destroyed masonary

NORTH

Metres

0 1 2 4 8

A hoard of currency bars was found on the edge of one of the pits in the alignment. It is presumed there would have been a visible hollow where the former pit was sited and the person who buried the bars used this as a marker for when they hoped to return and collect the bars. A total of 35 complete or broken bars survived *in situ* and a further 13 bars were scattered nearby when the overburden was stripped. Other bars may have been destroyed

5.12 Iron Age currency bars found at the edge of a pit from a pit alignment at Gretton.

by earlier ploughing. A few currency bars have been found in the county but hoards of this size are rare. The bars are believed to have been used as currency in the 1st century BC or early 1st century AD. There would obviously have been a long period of elapsed time between the construction and use of the pit alignment and deposition of the bars.

The Gretton alignment formed a T-junction with a ditch which ran at right angles to it. Although we found no evidence that the ditch was on the line of an earlier boundary – either a line of pits, or a natural feature such a hedge or edge of woodland – this is not an unreasonable assumption, especially as alignments have been discovered beneath ditches that were dug in the middle or late Iron Age (e.g. Wollaston). It seems likely that when the ditch was dug its upcast or bank sealed the first (or last) pit in the alignment (F40) as the filling in this pit was sterile and differed from that in other pits in the alignment. This may also explain why the currency bars were positioned on the edge of the second pit (F39), as the person who buried the bars may have thought they would be more easily recoverable if placed in a shallow hole adjacent to a bank.

The quarrying at Gretton began to the north-east of the village, close to the road to Harringworth, where the quarry manager at the time recalls seeing a large amount of burnt stones and other signs of occupation. The adjacent area is called Harborough Hill, which has the name 'borough' or 'bury' similar to other hillfort

5.13 Plan of southern end of pit alignment at Gretton.

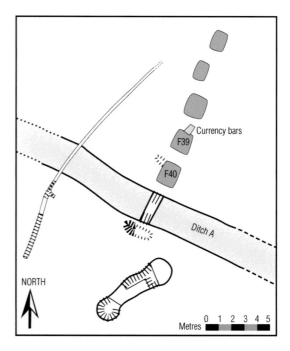

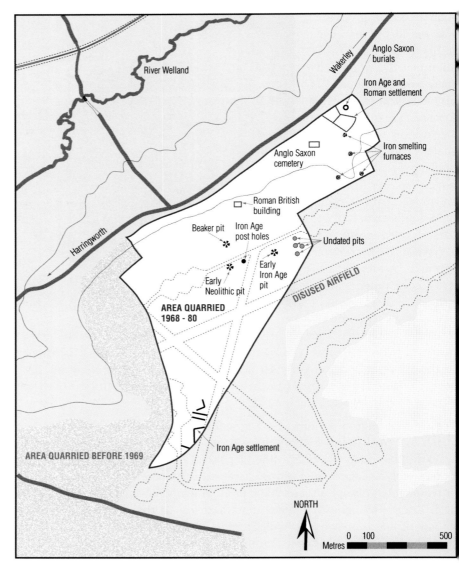

5.14 All sites in the Gretton/ Harringworth quarry area.

Anglo Saxon burials

Iron Age and Roman settlement

Iron smelting furnaces

River Welland

Wakerley

Anglo Saxon cemetery

Roman British building

Beaker pit

Iron Age post holes

Undated pits

Harringworth

Early Neolithic pit

Early Iron Age pit

DISUSED AIRFIELD

AREA QUARRIED 1968 - 80

AREA QUARRIED BEFORE 1969

Iron Age settlement

NORTH

0   100   500
Metres

sites in the county. It is possible therefore that an important Iron Age site was destroyed at that time.

Additional work was carried out in the Gretton/Harringworth area towards the end of the 1970s when further Iron Age features were revealed by soil stripping. At Gretton, two parallel ditches were found roughly 5-6 metres apart that may have flanked a trackway or droveway. There were several sherds of pottery on the surface and I realized the potential value of obtaining a pottery assemblage of this date. The ditches averaged over 1 metre in depth and, working alone, I excavated the ditch filling for around 70 metres using just a fork and trowel. I was able to excavate long sections of the ditch in one metre sections throwing the spoil forward into the competed area. I recovered 2,750 sherds of pottery and a number of objects made from iron, bone, shale, stone and clay. Radiocarbon dates from charcoal found in the ditches suggests they date to around the 5th–4th centuries BC.

A similar pattern of parallel ditches was also found at Harringworth, some 2 miles to the south-west of the Gretton features. These were associated with three other enclosure or boundary ditches and a number of pits and post holes. Pottery recovered from the upper filling of the ditches was dated to the 4th-3rd century BC and the ditches could have been contemporary with those at Gretton. The pottery from the latest phase of the site was dated to the 2nd or 1st century BC which suggests a long period of activity.

The wealth of archaeological sites discovered within the Gretton/Harringworth area was not dissimilar to that experienced at Aldwincle. This suggests that we were either extremely fortunate in uncovering relatively rare examples of extensive multi-period occupation or, as is more likely, that there are (or were) many similar areas in the county with evidence of intensive past activity that have not been subject to the same level of archaeological scrutiny.

Weekley

A second extensive Iron Age/Romano -British complex was excavated at Weekley, just north of Kettering, in the latter half of the 1970s. This was again carried out in advance of ironstone quarrying but in the event the quarry closed in 1980 with the result that a lot of the site now remains largely undisturbed.

Although it was known that there was a Roman villa on the site, it was aerial photographs taken by Dick Hollowell that identified the enclosures threatened by quarrying. Other enclosures and number of kiln sites were identified by Dr Tony Clark using a magnetometer in 1971. Trial trenches at that time suggested that the Roman villa may have been ploughed away or recorded in the wrong place but they did reveal a well preserved lime kiln which we subsequently excavated (see below).

The excavations at Weekley covered an area of approximately 2.5 hectares; 50 metres wide by 500 metres long running parallel to the quarry face. This revealed a series of ditched enclosures and evidence of continuous occupation from the 2nd century BC until the 2nd century AD. Although the adjacent villa was probably in use by the end of this period, there was little evidence of later Roman activity in the excavated area.

The earliest features consisted of a number of enclosures (Enclosure A, B, G, K and L) connected by a series of boundary or field ditches extending over 500 metres. This included a number of possible hut sites, one in Enclosures C and one unenclosed to the south-east of the site, plus a house site (supported by a large quantity of domestic refuse, including decorated pottery) in the area of Enclosure K. There were 32 small pits recorded, plus 14 which were clay lined, most of which included burnt stones thought to be have been used for heating water, perhaps for dyeing wool.

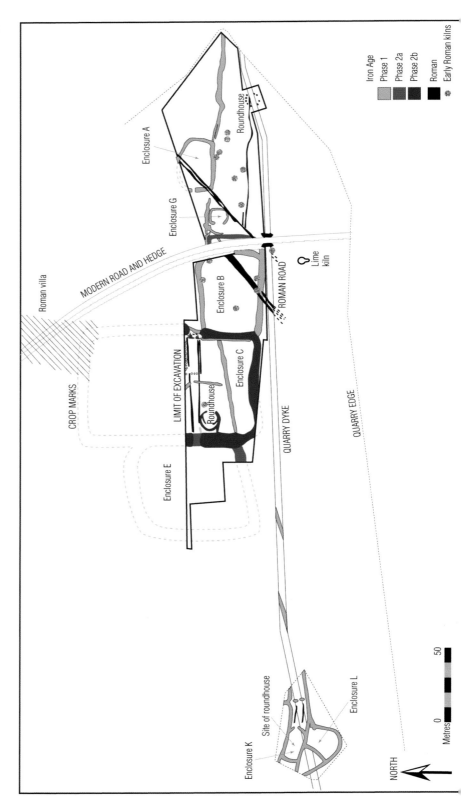

5.15 Plan of Iron Age and Roman site at Weekley.

Iron Age
Phase 1
Phase 2a
Phase 2b
Roman
Early Roman kilns

Roman villa

MODERN ROAD AND HEDGE

Enclosure A

Roundhouse

Enclosure G

Enclosure B

ROMAN ROAD

Lime kiln

CROP MARKS

LIMIT OF EXCAVATION

Enclosure C

Roundhouse

Enclosure E

QUARRY DYKE

QUARRY EDGE

Enclosure K

Site of roundhouse

Enclosure L

NORTH

Metres   0   50

The early part of the second phase of activity, during the later Iron Age and early Roman period, saw the existing Enclosures A and B both recut, and the creation of Enclosure E to the west. There were many post holes dating to this period which may represent evidence of occupation, but no definitive hut site was revealed. As this phase progressed, the earlier enclosure ditches gradually filled, and the focus of activity shifted towards a new area Enclosure C, situated between B and E and surrounded by a new deep ditch 3 metres deep. There was a stone causeway across the ditch on the western side of Enclosure C (which also ran across the adjacent ditch to Enclosure E) which was linked by a trackway to the main entrance of the eastern side of the compound. This entrance had a formidable gate-structure set in a series of large post-pits and trenches. There was a concentration of post holes and gullies situated on the western side of the enclosure which formed a distinct hut site with a number of different phases. In addition, there were three post hole groupings towards the south which may represent hut sites.

The final phase of activity dates to the first 150 years following the Roman Conquest. Enclosures C and E continued in use but no new enclosures were laid out during this period. The remains of 14 pottery kilns dating to the 1st century AD were widely distributed across the site, suggesting that pottery production was an important local industry which had developed over this time. Some of the kilns had stoking areas utilizing hollows above earlier enclosure ditches – and evidence was also found of a late Iron Age bonfire kiln constructed in a hollow of a partially filled ditch – and all the kilns were based on a single-flue updraught design, a common typology in the Nene Valley. The bonfire kiln represents rare evidence of pottery manufacture in the late Iron Age period.

Towards the end of this phase, when the kilns had gone out of use, activity probably shifted to the north of the excavated area towards the site of the villa.

FOLLOWING PAGES
5.17 (Left) Weekley, detailed plan of features in Enclosure C. Highlighted section shows area illustrated in adjacent photograph (5.18) .

5.18 (Right) Weekley, view looking westward into Enclosure C showing entrance in foreground and trackways.

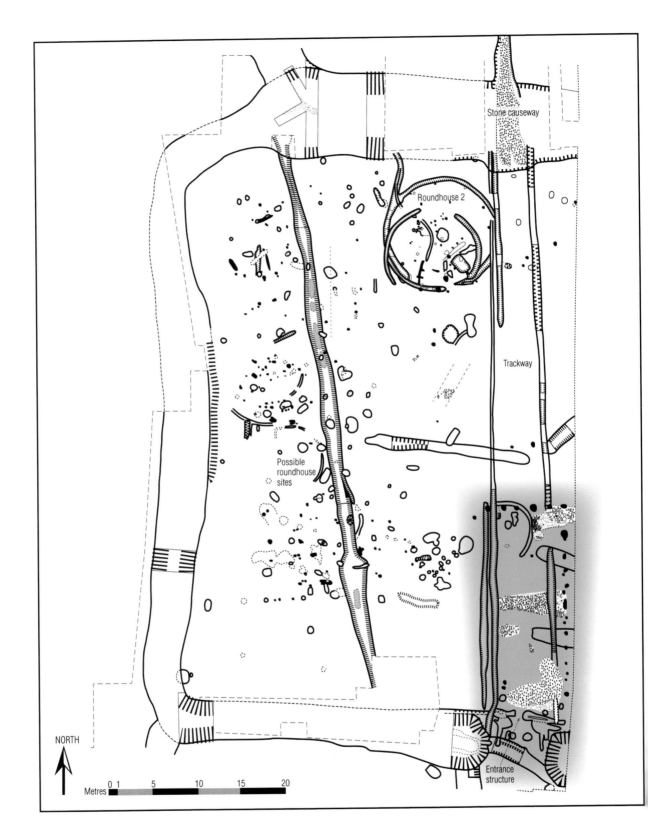

Stone causeway

Roundhouse 2

Trackway

Possible
roundhouse
sites

Entrance
structure

NORTH

Metres 0 1 5 10 15 20

While it is not possible to be certain when the villa was built, the lime kiln – which was probably used in its construction – was dated to around 160 AD. The kiln was 2.8 metres in diameter and had a long narrow flue leading to a stokehole, or working area which had previously acted as a quarry for the limestone to build the kiln. A Roman road was also constructed sometime during this period. It ran from the Roman settlement to the south-west into north Kettering towards a ford over the River Isle at Geddington. Parts of metalling survived where it had been protected by an adjacent hedge.

Analysis of the animal bones suggests that during the early phases of the site, sheep were the predominant species, bred for both wool and their meat, although pigs and cattle were also raised for their contribution to the meat supply. The occurrence of weaving implements, loomweights and clay-lined pits for dyeing is also consistent with the traditional pattern of animal husbandry during this time. During the later phases there was a growth in the use of cattle, both for meat and traction, and evidence of cereal production as well as other metal working crafts, all consistent with the range of activities likely to be carried out at a well appointed villa-farm complex.

5.19 Roman Lime Kiln at Weekley.

5.20 Example of La Tene decorated ware from Weekley (approx height 14cm).

The site was particularly significant because of the large assemblage of pottery and other small finds recovered. In particular, there were 366 sherds decorated with the familiar La Tene curvilinear or linear design that typifies high status sites during the middle-late Iron Age. Although similar pottery has been found on other sites in the county, this has never amounted to more than 20 sherds, which illustrates the potential importance of the site at Weekley. Most of this pottery is presumed to have been made locally, but there were some vessels imported from South West England which provides evidence of trade at this time. During the middle and later phases of the site, the ceramic assemblage changed and became more Romanised in both form and fabric. The overall pottery assemblage was particularly important in demonstrating the evolution of type and form during the transition from the Iron Age to the Roman period.

The quantity of decorated pottery recovered and the occurrence of vessels imported from South West England may suggest that the site was of some importance, possibly as a focus of wealth and power of the local tribe in the area. This is supported by the nature of the defences, with deep ditches and the elaborately constructed gateway. The extent to which this was a reflection of status or merely a defensive response to the threat of imperialist expansion of the Belgic kingdom from the south and south-east remains uncertain.

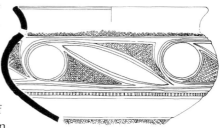

5.21 Example of of imported Glastonbury ware found at Weekley (approx height 10cm).

Sites in the Corby and Weldon Area

A number of other Iron Age sites were discovered in the Corby area during this period. This included two Iron Age sites found during housing development in 1974; a late Iron Age enclosure was excavated at the junction of Viking Way and Brandenburg Road and an early Iron Age ditch was sectioned at Stockholme Close in the same year. The late Ron Cross is said to have observed many archaeological features during the development of Corby in the 1960s, which were destroyed without record. This is particularly disappointing as most of the area was within Rockingham Forest during the medieval period and so early features may have been well preserved.

Just outside Corby, at Great Oakley, quarrying revealed features dated to the late Bronze Age-early Iron Age period (9th-6th century BC) making it one of the earliest recorded sites of this period. This included two structures, defined by semicircular gullies and a number of shallow pits. Of particular interest was the remains of an iron smelting furnace which may have been of a similar date as pieces of slag were found in one of the pits identical to those found in the furnace itself. Analysis has shown that the nearest source of the nodular ore used in the furnace was over one kilometre away. A watercourse now originates to the north of the site but during the quarrying it was found that it originally extended up to the site. Where it ran alongside the furnace, masses of furnace debris, including lining, had been discarded into the watercourse, suggesting that the furnace had been rebuilt and used many times.

5.22 Bronze Age urn from Weldon (approx height 12cm).

Another site was discovered on the ironstone quarries at Weldon. Soil stripping revealed a Bronze Age cemetery containing four inhumation burials and at least four cremations, with three small urns found amongst them. A limestone scatter was associated with the site

which had sunk into animal burrows but its presence may have indicated that the burials were originally under a stone cairn.

Further south at Geddington, the site of an Iron Age circular building, dated to the 2nd or 3rd century, was revealed in 1977. This was unusual because there were two elongated pits or short lengths of ditch in front of the entrance. It seems likely that they flanked an outer gateway which provided an extra barrier at the approach to the hut. The circular building overlay an earlier undated enclosure ditch.

Sites in the Nene Valley – Grendon and Ringstead

Although much of my work during this time was concentrated on the ironstone quarries in the north of the county, similar threats were bring presented by gravel extraction in the Nene Valley. A multi-period site at Grendon was not dissimilar to that excavated at Aldwincle, consisting of features dating from the Neolithic to the Iron Age. Work was carried out by others in the mid 1970s and I maintained a watching brief and carried out salvage work during the remainder of this period. Although aerial photographs showed extensive crop marks in the area being quarried, there was no finance available for detailed excavation.

Features recorded included two probable barrows with a number of pits close to the ring ditches containing four Bronze Age urns and an unusually long flint arrowhead; a series of five early pit alignments, traced for a distance of 550 metres; a series of 27 evenly spaced, spade dug trenches that was almost

5.24 Plan of pit alignments and lazy beds at Grendon.

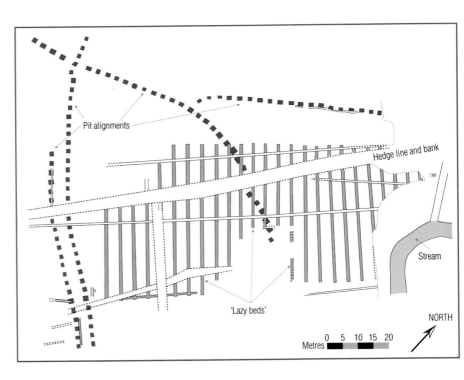

certainly the first known Roman vineyard in the area, and the remains of an Anglo-Saxon settlement including five sunken-floored buildings and the remains of two iron smelting furnaces.

Further north, a Roman building was revealed by gravel quarrying at Ringstead, just south of Thrapston. The excavated section of the building lies to the west of the modern road from Ringstead to Great Addington, with the remaining part undisturbed on the eastern side of the road. The excavation exposed the remains of a tessellated floor inside a circular building and part of a Jupitor column that had been discarded in a pit. We got unexpected support and assistance from the foreman at the quarry, Brian Pye, who turned out to be a keen collector of Roman coins. Unfortunately, (or perhaps fortunately) we were not able to satisfy his interest by finding any coins during the excavation.

Further work in the quarry over a period of time led to the discovery of a pit alignment with a complete early Iron Age pot in one of the pits. This was particularly exciting as it is very unusual to find such well preserved dating evidence within a pit alignment, especially as it confirmed the proposed time period for features of this type. It was also interesting that the pits were sealed with alluvial clay and there was no surviving evidence of the upcast from the pits, either alongside the alignment or within the surounding area

5.25 A Jupitor column from a Roman building at Ringstead (approx height 30cm).

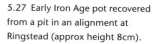

5.26 Pit alignment being excavated ahead of quarrying at Ringstead.

5.27 Early Iron Age pot recovered from a pit in an alignment at Ringstead (approx height 8cm).

End of the Decade – Brigstock

My final excavations during the 1970s were both on non quarry sites which reflected the changing nature of rescue archaeology at that time and provided an indication of where my future work would lie. At Brigstock an extremely well preserved Iron Age building, dating to the 2nd-1st century BC was discovered and excavated in 1979. The site had been in parkland in the medieval period and had escaped the damage caused by ridge and furrow cultivation. In addition, the building was sited in a small enclosure and the surviving low bank had given the interior of the site further protection from ploughing. The site was unusual as a stone path had been laid from the enclosure ditch to the front door of the house and other stone was found inside the building that may have supported bedding or furniture. Although it is not unknown for stone to be used on Iron Age sites, it has rarely survived on sites in Northamptonshire. The survival of the stone and a shallow wall trench were both features that may not have survived had the site been extensively ploughed. The work was carried out to fit in with the farming programme, and it was a pleasure to work on a site not surrounded by the noise and environmental destruction that I had become so used to on quarry sites.

5.28 Iron Age house site at Brigstock showing stonework in entranceway.

Finally, the base of an Anglo-Saxon building was revealed in house foundations at Stoke Doyle Road in Oundle. The finds contained both Roman and Anglo-Saxon material and the pottery assemblage from the 5th century AD was particularly significant.

More Report Writing

The number of excavations I had carried out since becoming a professional archaeologist meant that there was the ever-present danger of a backlog of post-excavation work, so I was keen to maintain progress on report writing in between work in the field. In addition to working in London, I also spent time at the Institute of Archaeology at Oxford. I was deeply indebted to one of Professor Cunliffe's assistants, Tim Ambrose, who provided much help on the publication on the reports of the Roman Bridge at Aldwincle and the Iron Age and Roman site at Wakerley. I was working intermittently on the latter for over four years and when it was finally published and occupied over 100 pages in the national journal 'Brittania' all the hard work seemed worth it. It was at this time that my name was put forward by Roger Goodburn, for election as a Fellow of the Society of Antiquaries (FSA), and I again felt enormously gratified that my work was recognized and appreciated within the archaeological community.

Brian Dix had helped on many of my excavations before he went to university, and I was fortunate that he was on hand later to help with the report on the important Iron Age and Roman sites at Weekley. This was a site that had been excavated over a number of years and for which a large amount of data had been accumulated. I found it disappointing that the final report only ran to 54 pages – with the rest produced as microfiche – as this did not seem to reflect the importance of the site and the amount of work that had gone into the excavation and report.

5.29 A busman's holiday to Butser Iron Age Farm in the 1970s (with Betty hiding behind a post).

However, as the decade drew to a close so did much of my work on the Northamptonshire ironstone quarries. It was not so apparent at the time but this was the end of a unique period of archaeological investigation in the county. It was a time when the wholesale destruction of landscapes through quarrying provided a unique opportunity for large scale open area excavations often covering multiple sites and multi-periods. But things were destined to change during the coming years, and to change far more than I ever envisaged.

CHAPTER SIX

1980s Onwards: The Later Period

"The present is the funeral of the past"

John Clare

The closure by British Steel of their ironstone working in the north of the county reduced the need for rescue excavations in this part of the county. However, it suited me to devote time to post-excavation work and for the early part of the decade most of my time was spent continuing my report writing on the excavations carried out in previous years, and carrying out limited evaluations and watching briefs on a number of sites across the county. Later on during this period I excavated an important Roman industrial site at Laxton and an Iron Age site at Stanwell Spinney, Wellingborough. Following a house move to the south of Northampton, I excavated Iron Age features to the south of Hunsbury hillfort.

Northamptonshire Archaeology Unit

Circumstances had already changed during the later part of the 1970s with the establishment of the Northamptonshire Archaeology Unit by the County Council. Although I was then paid through the council and technically under the management of the County Archaeologist, I remained self-employed and largely responsible for my own work to the Department of the Environment (who had taken over from the former Ministry of Works in the early 1970s), and subsequently English Heritage, who continued to pay me.

Relationships between myself and the then County Archaeologist, Alan Hannan, and his assistant Glenn Foard, were never as good as they might have been. Although I was based in the Unit, I was rarely consulted and never made to feel part of the set-up nor valued for my practical experience and knowledge of the county. It may be that people thought my methods were outdated and I was incapable of change, and I probably felt that the Unit was becoming too academic and theoretical.

Alan Hannan thought it was right that I should be paid at a scale below many of the new project officers – because they had degrees – despite my years of experience, which clearly did not help relationships. This was never considered when I retired and I was refused any pension or redundancy payments by Alan and the county council, which was in marked contrast to the treatment of staff by the development corporations. In the early 1980s, English Heritage did offer me the chance to become a permanent salaried member of the Unit – which would have been financially advantageous in the long run - but I declined because of the unsatisfactory nature of my relationship with the County Archaeologist.

Despite these difficulties, I carried out a number of limited excavations and watching briefs for the Unit during the early 1980s. This included early work on the Roman villa site at Stanwick; investigation of the likely damage caused by the BBC wireless station to the Iron Age hillfort at Daventry; assessment of development on Chapel Brampton golf course and at the Towcester cinema site. Watching briefs were carried out on a number of housing and road development sites including Brigstock, Byfield, Ditchford, Great Harrowden, Islip, Little Houghton, Rothersthorpe, Stanion, Wollaston, Yardley Hastings and Yardley Gobion. At two sites, Laxton and Stanwell Spinney, this led to further excavations.

Stanwick

At Stanwick, I carried out a limited excavation ahead of the major work carried out as part of the Raunds Area Project by English Heritage Central Excavation Unit between 1984 and 1991. This initial work suggested that Iron Age and Roman activity was not just confined to the known villa site, but extended over a number of fields covering a very large area. It also suggested that a thick soil cover would need to be removed that had all been disturbed by ploughing. I demonstrated this by siting a trial trench over a mosaic pavement, which illustrated the position of the pavement and also showed that it had been damaged by plough furrows despite the thick soil cover. The excavations subsequently carried out at Stanwick were the largest ever undertaken in the county at that time. The amount of finds and data recovered from the site was such that a report has still not been published.

Laxton

At Laxton, a re-alignment of the A43 trunk road revealed a major Roman iron-working site as well as evidence of occupation and a substantial inhumation cemetery. As no financial provision had been made for any archaeological investigation, the Highways Department of the County Council facilitated this by delaying work and agreeing to absorb the cost of rescue work within their budget.

Initially, the site looked beyond rescue and a number of visitors supported this view; Professor Tylecote even thought that there was so much slag that it must have come from the modern furnaces at Corby. The County Archaeologist visited the site and suggested that work should be concentrated on the cemetery. I disagreed because I knew the large furnaces were unique and potentially more important. Given the limited time and resources – I had one assistant, Steve Young, but most of the work was done by volunteers – I decided to carry out a limited excavation of the cemetery area but concentrate most of our effort on

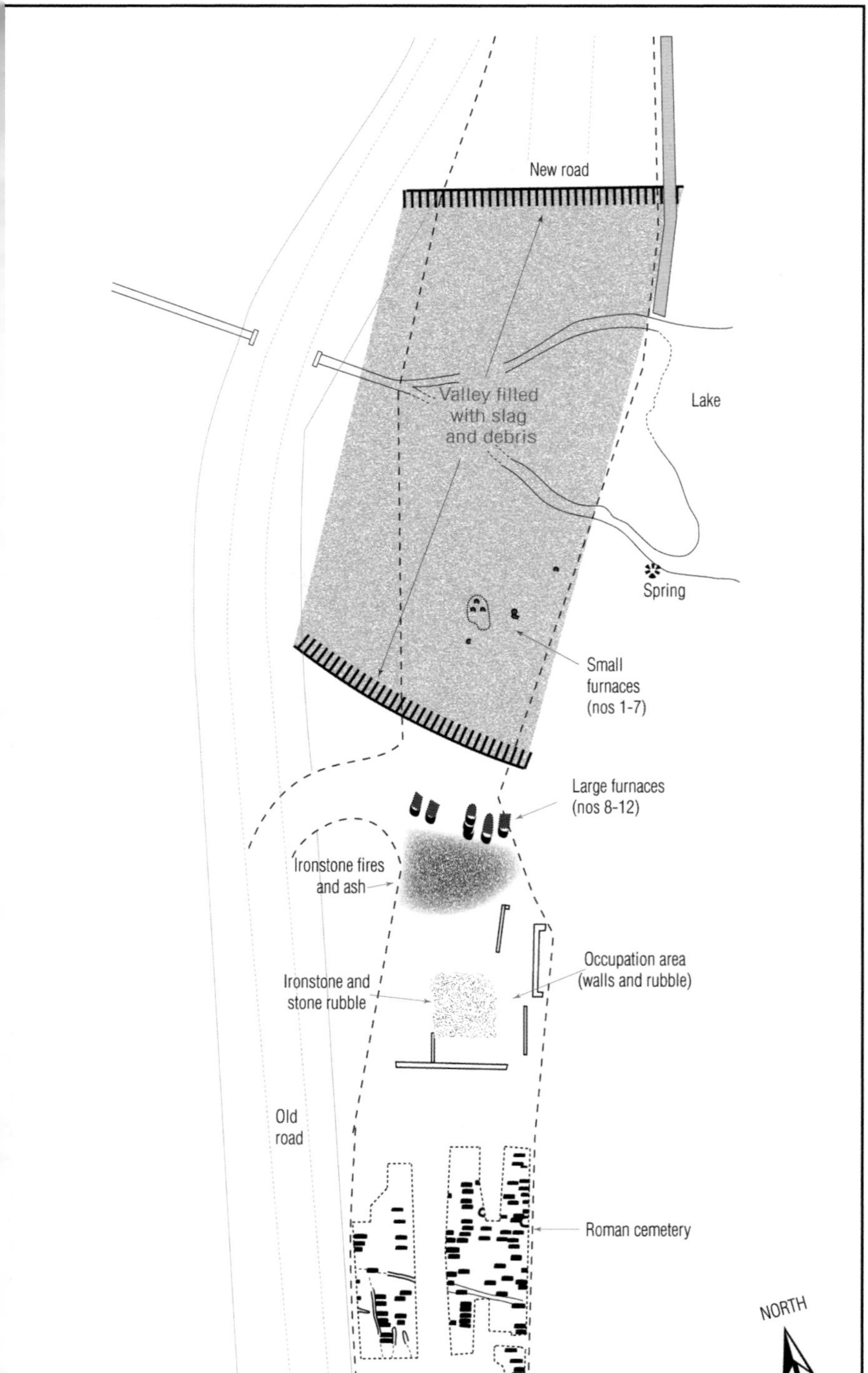

6.1 Plan of Laxton Roman iron working site.

New road

Valley filled with slag and debris

Lake

Spring

Small furnaces (nos 1-7)

Large furnaces (nos 8-12)

Ironstone fires and ash

Occupation area (walls and rubble)

Ironstone and stone rubble

Old road

Roman cemetery

NORTH

Laxton Lodge

0   30
Metres

the row of furnaces. I am indebted to Gill Johnston and Pat Foster for the many hours they spent helping to excavate the site and record the furnaces.

The site was situated on a north-facing slope with a valley at the bottom. A line of unusually large iron smelting furnaces was found near the bottom of the slope and the valley bottom was filled with slag and furnace debris. Above the line of the furnaces there was a substantial burnt area, presumably where the ore and charcoal was prepared for smelting. Above this area there were the remains of buildings or walls, and above this, the remains of the cemetery.

Excavation revealed that iron working had been carried out during two phases, with a row of exceptionally large furnaces being used during the early stages, which were eventually replaced with smaller conventional shaft furnaces in the later years. There were at least five large furnaces in use during the first phase, each of which was up to 1.5 metres in diameter internally, compared to an average size of around 0.3 metres for Roman smelting furnaces elsewhere. We managed to fully excavate two of the large furnaces (Furnaces 8 and 9) and a number of the smaller furnaces used during the second phase. These were found under the slag and furnace debris and the furnace builders had obviously dug pits into the slag and debris, filled the hole with clay and constructed furnaces in the clay filling.

6.2 One of the large iron smelting furnaces at Laxton after excavation.

Only limited work was carried out in the area of the adjacent settlement but this suggested it was originally a working area associated with the iron working, which was later built over with stone walls. The occupation debris indicated a likely settlement site and the pottery remains suggested occupation in the 2nd –3rd centuries AD. A total of 87 graves were recorded in the road corridor, but allowing for the areas that could not be examined, the total probably exceeded a hundred.

Iron working at Laxton appears to have been carried out on a massive scale compared to other known sites in the region, with the earlier and larger furnaces being unique to Roman Britain. However, so many questions remain unanswered about the ownership and control of the iron working process and the associated management of woodlands, transport etc that would also have been an important part of this process. It is possible that iron working began in the 1st century and occupation automatically followed. The dating evidence – including coins and extensive cemetery – certainly suggest that occupation or activity continued during most of the Roman period.

It was frustrating to see so much of this potentially important site destroyed without proper excavation and with so little record, especially as so many resources had been invested in the Archaeology Unit for exactly this purpose. I consoled myself with the knowledge that much of the site continued, and would remain secure in the small field to the east of the roadway, but I was dismayed when told later by the farmer that he had deep-ploughed the field and removed much stonework. Part of the area was also later destroyed to improve a fishing lake. I could not understand why more effort was not made to schedule the field after our excavations had revealed the importance of the site.

When work was completed on the road one of the furnaces which had been revealed in 1985 was positioned under the roadside verge. In 1998 I learnt that Anglian Water planned to dig a service trench along the verge and I received permission to excavate the furnace in advance of this work. I invited Peter Crew from Snowdonia National Park, who is an expert on the scientific aspects of iron working, to help with the excavation. This time we had no shortage of helpers but only a small trench alongside the road to accommodate them. The plan of the furnace was similar to those we had excavated earlier and a lot of samples were removed for scientific examination. When the service trench was eventually opened they crossed to the other side of the road before reaching the furnace so the structure should remain undisturbed.

6.3 Returning to excavate another furnace at Laxton in 1998.

Stanwell Spinney, Wellingborough

A watching brief at Stanwell Spinney, Wellingborough during this time also led to further excavation. This was an Iron Age settlement sited on the route of the new north-west bypass of the town. The site was previously known through aerial photography and I was particularly interested in a small spring close to the site known as Stanwell Spring, which I thought may have been an early sacred site with a shrine. It was possible to interpret a faint crop mark adjacent to the spring as an enclosure, but unfortunately the depth of soil in the valley and the stripping method used at the roadworks preventing any detailed examination of the site.

6.5 Stanwell Spinney, entranceway after excavation showing depth of ditch .

We did, however, excavate a D-shaped enclosure, sited on higher ground some 100 metres to the north which could have been a ritual site. The straight side of the D overlooked and faced the site of the spring and the only feature in the enclosure was a large hole which could have either supported a post or a large stone. This was positioned adjacent to the ditch midway along the straight side. In its earliest phase the ditch only enclosed an area some 9 metres by 7 netres but this was subsequently re-cut on a number of occasions. There was no evidence that the enclosure had a domestic function and it is hard to see why the people who used the enclosure needed a surrounding ditch one metre deep on well drained limestone. Other features we excavated on the site included the gateway to a deep-ditched oval enclosure, defined as a Wootton Hill type (see overleaf) and a number of pits. A human burial, consisting of a female aged 25-35, was found buried close to one of the pits.

A New Home

For a short while in the mid-1980s, archaeology took a back-seat as my wife and I planned and subsequently organised the building of a new house on a development adjacent to the park that contains the well-known hillfort at Hunsbury. I was never sure that my family and friends fully believed that this location was merely co-incidental; but in truth, it was a time when the southern area of the town was being rapidly developed and most self-build opportunities were in this area.

I was aware that our house plot was situated roughly midway between the hillfort and the known location of a Roman bathouse and therefore kept a constant look out for archaeological features throughout the early ground work on the site. Although I was keen to find any evidence of past activity, I was also aware that if the building inspector found signs of unstable ground, it would probably require deeper foundations costing extra money. I therefore had a combined sense of excitement and trepidation when, with my practiced eye, a saw a Iron Age ditch running straight through one of the main foundation trenches, just before the building inspector was due. Fortunately, he did not spot the ditch, and having resisted the urge to jump in the trench and start excavating, I quickly arranged for the trenches to be filled with concrete. However, after we had sold the house and when passing some 15 years later, I noticed a large crack in the external brickwork directly above where the ditch had been. Needless to say, I did not knock on the door and introduce myself.

Once the house was finished it provided an ideal location for monitoring archaeological remains revealed by housing development in the area. A number of early Iron Age features were found nearby when the new County Record Office was built at Mereway. The features were revealed in section around the sides of a large basement pit that exists beneath the present building. Later I excavated a number of early Iron Age pits when houses were built to the south of the Record Office, so the site is clearly extensive.

Wootton Hill Farm

A previously unknown Iron Age enclosure with a deep ditch was discovered at Wootton Hill Farm. The site lies on a spur some 400 metres to the south-west of Hunsbury hillfort with extensive views to the south and south-west, an outlook not possible from the fort. A similar deep double-ditched enclosure was also found at Briar Hill to the north of the fort in a similar topographical position. This raises questions about whether either or both of these sites were satellite enclosures or look out forts for the larger hillfort at Hunsbury.

Excavation at Wootton Hill Farm revealed that an earlier ditch predated the main enclosure, suggesting that an earlier enclosure may have existed to the south. The later enclosure ditch was dug to a consistently deep level, averaging about 2.6 metres. The entrance to the enclosure was on the west and associated with it were a series of trenches and post holes, including a pair of long post pits or stockade trenches containing limestone slabs, some 2 metres inside the ditch and 2 metres apart. These are likely to have held posts supporting an internal gateway, possibly attached to a stockade or timber revetment providing additional stability and defence. Alternatively, these features may have been

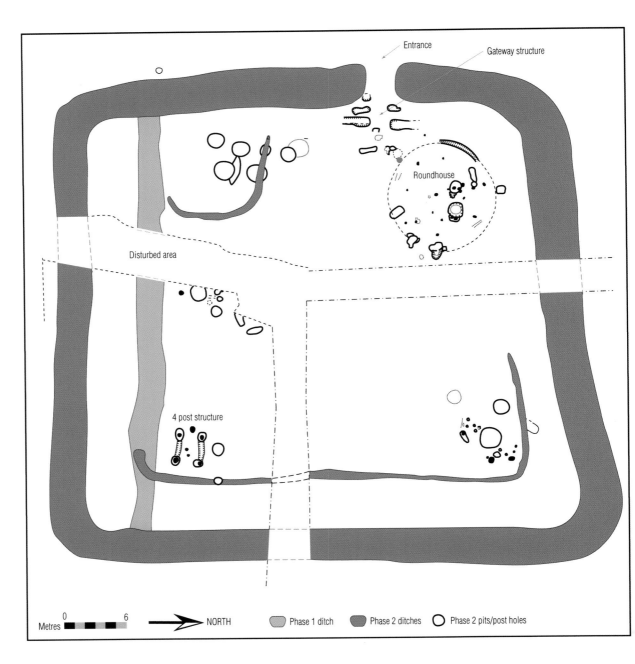

Phase 1 ditch	Phase 2 ditches		Phase 2 pits/post holes

Metres 0 ▬▬▬ 6 →NORTH

Entrance
Gateway structure
Roundhouse
Disturbed area
4 post structure

6.6 Plan of Iron Age enclosure at Wootton Hill Farm.

associated with a platform above the rampart overlooking the approach to the fort and providing a lookout or fighting platform.

On the left hand side of the entrance there was a small roundhouse or perhaps guard room, defined by a concentration of post holes and the remains of a wall trench. The entrance faced south-east, looking towards a small pen and a number of pits rather than the nearby entrance to the enclosure itself. In the south-east corner of the enclosure there was a four-post structure measuring

6.7 Deep enclosure ditch at Wootton Hill Farm.

3 metres by 2.5 metres which was interpreted as a possible lookout tower. There were a number of smaller postholes, both inside and outside the structure, which may have been ladder slots and supporting struts for the tower.

Whether the Wootton Hill Farm site, and that at Briar Hill, were satellite enclosures of Hunsbury hillfort or were independent sites each representing a stage in the development of individual farmsteads and local settlement drift remains uncertain. The pottery from Wootton Hill was certainly similar to much of the material from the hillfort and the two sites are therefore likely to have been in contemporary use at some stage in the Iron Age (the ceramics suggest that this was probably in the 2nd or 1st centuries BC.) The combination of deep ditch, possible passageway entrance and guard house and lookout tower provides good evidence that the enclosure was designed for defence and, if contemporary with the hillfort, the topographical position would strongly support the satellite hypothesis.

An Anglo-Saxon iron smelting furnace was revealed on a housing estate to the south of the hillfort and prior to its discovery a new public house had been built just across the road, strangely called 'The Viking'. The assemblage of pottery from the hillfort at Hunsbury contains over a hundred sherds of Anglo-Saxon date, so it is perhaps not surprising to find evidence of activity nearby.

Hunsbury, Northampton

Living so close, it was inevitable that I would also investigate conditions at Hunsbury hillfort itself. A large part of the interior of the fort had been quarried for ironstone in the 19th century, which removed much of the inner edge of the rampart. Since that time further deterioration has been caused by weathering, a large rabbit population and by the behaviour of youngsters within what is a public park. I tried to emphasize the need for some sort of management plan to conserve what remains as one of the county's most important archaeological sites, but neither English Heritage nor Northampton Borough Council were prepared to take responsibility – each arguing that it was the other party's job.

6.8 Section excavated through the bank at Hunsbury hillfort.

In 1998, with the assistance of Alan Williams, I excavated a 7 metre section through the rampart on the north side of the fort. A section dug previously by Professor Atkinson near the southeast entrance, in an area not disturbed by quarrying, showed that the rampart had two phases. The section we excavated had been truncated by quarrying and erosion and it was unclear whether there were originally two phases. The rampart we excavated was of box construction with the rear supported by a stout stockade and the whole bound together with horizontal timbers. The front of the rampart had not survived but stone may have been used for revetment in addition to posts. The rampart was some 3 metres wide and at some stage was burnt down in what appears to have been a massive fire. Radiocarbon dates from the charred wood suggests it was constructed between the 7th and 5th centuries BC. Northampton Borough Council was supportive throughout our work but it was disappointing that the Archaeology Unit showed little interest despite the fort being less than a mile from their office.

Later, in 2003, I received a grant from the Parkinson's Disease Society, under a scheme called *'Create It'* to carry out further research on the hillfort and together with Martin Tingle we organized a number of projects in the area over the following four years. This included a botanical survey; which identified ways to manage the existing vegetation; and two geophysical surveys; one of which located the quarry edge and sought to identify remaining features in the unquarried area, and another which covered the whole of the rampart and confirmed that evidence of burning occurred around most of the circuit.

In addition, we dug trenches in the interior which showed that the unquarried area was, on average, 10 metres wider than on the plan drawn by the Royal Commission. We also made three machine cuts to remove the eroded material from the inner face of the rampart which showed that it survived to a height of between 1.0-1.8 metres around the circuit. Further work was carried out in the interior in late 2007, which located a large pit, possibly a quarry pit, and other features just inside the rampart.

I find it extremely regrettable that the hillfort has been allowed to deteriorate to such an extent and that no public body has taken proper responsibility for its preservation and maintenance. It is now over 20 years since I first tried to get the ramparts preserved since when further deterioration now means they are probably not worth conserving. Neither the authorities nor the people of Northampton have properly appreciated the value of this historic site and it will soon be too late to retain much of its original form and character.

6.9 Hunsbury hillfort in the 1960s surrounded by countryside.

6.10 Hunsbury hillfort in the 1990s in the middle of an urban landscape.

Commercial Archaeology

Relations between myself and the County Archaeologist got no better during the remainder of the 1980s. At this time it seemed that Alan Hannan had his own agenda and set of priorities that did not include any involvement with, or contribution from, myself. Things came to a head in the late 1980s when an outsider who had little practical experience or knowledge of the county was appointed to oversee potentially important work along the new A14 roadway. It was clear that I would not be given any future work by the Unit and this was confirmed in 1988 when a letter from the County Archaeologist informed me that I was no longer based in the Unit and could not use their offices or facilities. This meant that at the age of 60 and after 25 years dedicated service to the archaeology of Northamptonshire I was effectively out of work and with no income. Moreover, I was refused any redundancy pay or claim to a pension as the county council insisted I had been self employed throughout my period attached to the Unit.

At this time, the publication of PPG16[25] was gradually transforming the way in which archaeological work was carried out. The introduction of the *'developer pays'* principle and the subsequent opening up of the market for archaeological work meant that county archaeology units no longer had a monopoly position within their respective areas. Much has, of course, been written about the subsequent advantages and disadvantages of this development, especially its possible impact on the independence of the archaeologist and the subsequent integrity of the archaeological investigation. One consequence was that the Archaeology unit was divided into two – a curatorial section, to give planning advice and to monitor fieldwork, and a contracts section to tender for work in competition with others.

In my position, I had little option but to seek work as an independent contractor, and together with Alan Williams, a long-time friend and valued colleague, we tendered for work within the county. Because of our experience and low overheads we often managed to undercut the Contracts Section of the Archaeology Unit and won seven contracts over the next two years. However, the Curatorial Section of the Unit retained responsibility for assuring the quality of our work and the officer who carried out this task wrote letters to the developers complaining about the quality of our work. I thought this was very unfair as our work was in no way inferior and with our experience we were frequently able to extract the maximum information from a site at minimum cost. Fortunately, my experience, knowledge and track record was sufficiently well-known for people to realize just how unjustifiable these comments were.

Thrapston

One of the first contracts we undertook was back in my home territory of Thrapston. At that time the town was being extended eastwards over a known Iron Age circular enclosure adjacent to a newly built service station on the A14. I was asked to evaluate the site and was surprised to find the enclosure dated to the late Bronze-early Iron Age period (9th–6th century BC). Known sites of this period are rare in the county and circular enclosures of this nature are rare nationally. A full excavation of the threatened half of the enclosure was subsequently carried out by Thames Valley Archaeological Services for whom I provided a pottery report.

FINA Pipeline

In 1990 an oil pipeline was being laid by FINA running across the whole county from Wakerley in the north to Hargreave in the south. The Wessex Archaeological Trust had a national contract for this work and I was employed to carry out a watching brief on the Northamptonshire section. The trench was not open for long making it difficult to record features in section and I had to rely on the corridor stripped of topsoil being clean enough to expose features in the bedrock. Nevertheless a number of features were identified including a Roman pottery kiln and aisled barn at Wakerley; late Iron Age and Roman features at Deenethorpe; a filled-in well at Lyveden deserted medieval village and another late Iron Age and Roman site to the east of Raunds. Overall, although the pipeline was routed to miss known sites, it was surprising that relatively few new sites were discovered.

Towcester

At Towcester, we excavated Roman defences in the backyard of No 158 (The Masonic Yard) to locate the base of the Roman town wall and recorded a section of the rampart and area behind it. The rampart was at least 12 metres wide and it sealed a trample of mortar associated with the building of the wall.

Wollaston

A large scale evaluation was commissioned by Pioneer Aggregates in 1990 in advance of gravel extraction at Wollaston. The evaluation covered eight fields and an area of 4,000 square metres was examined using around 120 trenches. An extensive pattern of crop marks had been recorded from the air and the challenge was to locate trenches in the key areas. These had to be measured from estimated positions in the hedgerow and we had to struggle through wild vegetation to get to the right spot. It was gratifying that we were one hundred percent successful in our trench locations.

The majority of features showing as crop marks were Iron Age in date and consisted of a series of enclosures or small farms aligned roughly along a contour parallel to the River Nene. The pottery suggests they date mainly to the middle Iron Age (4th–2nd centuries BC), but the earliest features were numerous pit alignments. In contrast, a series of parallel trenches, of Roman date, were later found to contain vine pollen.

I was later invited by the gravel company to tender for the full excavation but declined because of the lack of support and the criticism I knew I would receive from the Curatorial Section of the Archaeology Unit. The Contracts Section of the Unit eventually carried out the full excavation, but it is disappointing that a report has still not been published some 15 years after work began and 9 years after the final phase of work.

Borough Hill, Daventry

In the late 1920s the BBC constructed a transmitting station on Borough Hill, Daventry, a large and well known hillfort. The hillfort is one of the largest in the country, extending over 45 hectares, and the BBC's installations extended over much of this area, within the fort and outside the defences to the south and south-west. When they planned to replace many installations in the early 1990s I was commissioned to carry out an archaeological evaluation in advance of this work.

The plan was to build 27 new four-legged towers and we excavated a 4 metre square trench at the base of one leg in each tower. In addition we excavated a number of trenches where the ground would also be disturbed and investigated several known archaeological features on the hilltop. Our evaluations showed that features were widespread across the area with those of early Iron Age date concentrated along the sheltered south and east sides of the fort. The work was carried out in the winter of 1991, but by the summer of that year all rebuilding plans had been abandoned. All but one of the masts have now been dismantled.

6.11 BBC transmitting station built on site of an Iron Age hillfort at Borough Hill, Daventry.

End of a Career

My last 'professional' work was carried out for the Commission for New Towns in 1992 in the south-west of Northampton. Housing development was planned in the area and an archaeological assessment was carried out over 14 fields covering 74 hectares. A number of trial trenches were excavated to the south-east of Upton mill where two possible barrows were situated. However, the first turned out to be a natural gravel island, and the second was probably the site of a medieval windmill. Other trenches were dug where trackway ditches and a small enclosure were known from the air. The enclosure ditch was found to be 1.7 metres deep and filled with a dark loamy soil. This would be unusual in a Bronze Age context but has parallels in the ditches of the Neolithic monument at Aldwincle and other sites.

The changing nature of archaeological work in the country – brought about largely by PPG16 – meant that by this time various bodies, such as the Institute of Field Archaeologists (IFA), were introducing national frameworks and guidelines setting out practices and standards for archaeological investigation. The County Archaeologist, Alan Hannan, interpreted this advice to mean it was necessary to have an archaeological qualification at degree level to be able to direct excavations. Not surprisingly, I disagreed strongly with this, and argued that with almost 30 years' practical experience, and a growing number of published reports, someone such as myself – also with membership of the Society of Antiquaries – should not be precluded from tendering for archaeological contracts. This failed to change their policy and I terminated my membership with the IFA on a question of principle. As soon as the County Archaeologist learnt that I was no longer a member of the IFA I was taken off the list of approved contractors in 1993.

So, as I reached retirement age at 65, it was with some sadness that I realized my career as a professional archaeologist had come to an end. I have of course continued my interest in archaeology since then. In particular, I have maintained a keen interest in the chronology of local Iron Age pottery and have continued to write pottery reports for other people's excavations. I have also worked as a volunteer on various sites including Iron Age sites at Crick (Daventry International Rail Freight Terminal) and Rothersthorpe, and carried out the further work described earlier at Hunsbury hillfort. I have never lost my interest in holes in the ground and in 2001 found at unknown Roman villa on a housing estate at Wootton.

I did complete all of my post-excavation reports during the 1990s, and in total, including those where I was co-author, I published 36 reports in the 32 years between 1969 and 2000. Seven of these reports were published in national journals and the remaining in the local journal Northamptonshire Archaeology. It is with some pride and a strong sense of personal satisfaction that I look back on this work and the contribution that I hope it has made to archaeology in the county. If at least the Jackson ancestors (hopefully looking down from above) think my efforts in the soil have been as worthy as theirs, and if Miss Norma Whitcome, (whether she is still with us or not), also thinks her efforts were worthwhile then I am content.

6.12 Late Bronze Age socketed axe found at Daventry (approx size 10cm).

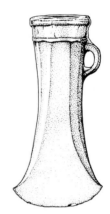

6.13 Back at Hunsbury hillfort aged 80, watchin Robert Moore do all the work.

6.14 OVERLEAF
Reconstruction drawing of Wootton Hill Farm enclosure by Alex Thompson.

PART THREE

Post-Excavation Reports

CHAPTER SEVEN

An Archaeologist Looks Back

"If life had a second edition, how I would correct the proofs"
John Clare

When looking back on any part of one's life it is often necessary to suppress the nostalgia gene that is constantly telling us how much better things were in the past. When there was no hooliganism or anti social behaviour and when all communities lived in peace and tranquiltity[26]. This, of course, is as far from the truth as is the notion that the rescue archaeologist was some form of county-based Indiana Jones bravely rescuing sites from destruction from under the teeth of mechanical diggers and excavators.

In practice, rescue archaeology in the 1960s and 70s was often a difficult and lonely existence with little support either in terms of resources or from the authorities. Moreover, it was usually necessary to work seven days a week, through all weathers, and often in isolated and inhospitable situations. And although some quarry managers were helpful, some were distrustful and even aggressive on occasions if they thought you threatened their progress. But it was also an existence that provided great personal and professional freedom; a clearly-defined sense of purpose and archaeological integrity, and a great deal of personal satisfaction and reward (albeit non-financial). I do not think I could have achieved this in any other walk of life or enterprise.

7.1 The typical working environment during most of my archaeological career, here at Ringstead gravel quarry (the sun was not always shining).

An Inspector from English Heritage once said that I had green fingers when it came to finding important sites. If this was so, it was only because I had complete freedom to visit the quarry sites and, where necessary, investigate archaeological features as and when they were being revealed. This was as much about luck and being in the right place at the right time as it was about anything else. For example, at Aldwincle, there were no surface indications or crop marks to indicate the presence of the Neolithic mortuary enclosure and it was only while plotting some Iron Age ditches at gravel level that we realized one of them was a complete circle and probably an early prehistoric barrow. Similarly, it was fortunate that we were working at Thrapston when the section of the Roman bridge was briefly revealed in the quarry face. The frightening corollary of this is the number of sites that have been and/or continue to be destroyed without record because people are not fortunate enough to be in the right place at the right time.

The right place: right time approach to excavation is of course largely determined by happenstance. A more controllable influence on the efficacy of archaeological investigation is to make sure that excavation is carried out using the right tools and right techniques. Ideally, stripping top soil down to the right level with a mechanical scraper will expose archaeological features without destroying them. There are occasions when it is as simple as this; for example, as I walked behind the box scraper at Wakerley and recovered human bones scattered over the area it was clear we had a Saxon cemetery site. Similarly, many other archaeological features and sites were revealed on the Wakerley/Corby quarries as scrapers exposed the limestone bedrock.

There may be occasions, however, where mechanical cleaning gives a false impression that an area is devoid of archaeological features. For example, at Weekley Hall Wood, an area seemed reasonably clean after scraping with just one post hole revealed. However, further detailed cleaning by trowel and brush exposed another 98 post holes forming 4-post and other structures of early Iron Age date. Even careful cleaning may not always reveal all the features. At Wakerley, we located a number of Iron Age houses and each had a number of internal posts to support the roof. It was only after measuring the spacing between those post holes that were initially revealed that the full ring of posts was subsequently discovered.

Deciding when to use a mechanical digger and when to use hand tools is of course a key decision, especially when faced with a large site and a small labour force. Good forward planning is often required to make the best use of these differing resources while optimizing the chances of recovering and recording archaeological features. For example, at Weekley, we identified an enclosure where there appeared to be only a scatter of internal features, and exposed this by using a JCB once a week to strip as much overburden as possible. For the following week we excavated and planned any features in this strip, thereby allowing the following week's soil to be dumped in the newly excavated (and recorded) area. This saved a lot of time moving soil and restoring the land and also led to a detailed record of the features in the area.

Planning activity based on forecast weather patterns and the prevailing geological conditions is also important if the best use is to be made of the time available. A clay bedrock is often difficult to clean when dry, but is much easier if tackled in the early morning after rain or even a heavy dew (if early enough). Again, in the winter time it is always possible to excavate ditch sections if they are kept covered overnight. Not always comfortable, but an archaeologist's lot is ever thus.

The choice of the right hand tool for the conditions can also affect the efficacy of the excavation process. Although the mattock and shovel are the most commonly used tools on excavations, I always found a two pronged hoe (Canterbury hoe) and a wide-pronged fork to be more efficient in breaking up soil. The Canterbury hoe is particularly useful for loosening redeposited material that often occurs on quarry sites. When it comes to cleaning large areas, an entrenching tool used on its side, can be as effective as a trowel but much more efficient. At Wakerley, the bedrock was rubbly or decayed limestone and a very large area was hand cleaned using only an entrenching tool, trowel and stiff brush.

Despite my years spent in the field, I am still puzzled why some archaeological features show as crop marks and others do not. For example, at Weekley, the aerial photograph of the Iron Age and Romano-British site was accurately

7.2 Iron Age/Romano-British settlement at Weekley. Aerial photograph (left) and excavated plan (right).

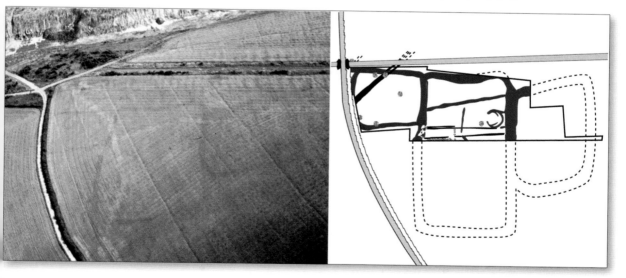

reflected in the later plan obtained by thorough excavation. Conversely, there have been many sites only discovered by excavation because there has been no prior knowledge from survey work. For example, at Aldwincle, there were two early Bronze Age barrows, and the Neolithic mortuary enclosure, roughly aligned and close together, yet the barrow ditches could be seen from the air and the enclosure and numerous Iron Age ditches could not. Similarly, the extensive Iron Age and Roman site excavated at Wakerley had not been recorded from the air despite having a thin soil cover and permeable bedrock. It is also interesting that fieldwalking the area in advance of quarrying produced nothing to indicate the presence of a major site. Perhaps a timely reminder of the variable nature of survey work and that it does not always reveal as much archaeological activity as we often assume it does.

Looking back, the most rewarding excavations were either those that yielded new information about the past, or where the type of site was rare if not unique at the time. In chronological terms this includes the Neolithic and Bronze Age sites at Aldwincle, Earls Barton and Grendon; the Iron Age sites at Twywell, Brigstock, Wootton Hill Farm and Stanwell Spinney, plus the various sites of pit alignments; the late Iron Age/Roman sites at Weekley and Wakerley; the Roman bridge at Aldwincle and iron smelting furnaces at Laxton, and the Anglo-Saxon cemetery at Wakerley.

If I ever had the luxury of correcting the proofs for Clare's Second Edition, there are a number of sites where I regret that things were not done differently, either before, during or after the excavation. Foremost, is the sad fate of the Roman timbers from the bridge at Aldwincle. These were massive timbers found in excellent condition, lying above gravel that was not worth quarrying anyway. The quarry company would have been happy to quarry around the site and leave the bridge protected *in situ*. Instead, quarrying continued, the structure was destroyed and the timbers were taken to a Ministry of Works depot at Kirby Hall, where they were allowed to rot away. Given that the Thrapston quarry is now a popular visitor spot – albeit covered by water – it is sad there is nothing to mark the existence of the site when, (admittedly in hindsight), there was such potential to retain either the original or a reconstruction of the bridge.

7.3 Roman bridge reconstruction in the Rheinisches Landesmuseum, Bonn, Germany. This may have been similar to the bridge at Aldwincle.

The second excavation I was unhappy with was the important Roman industrial site at Laxton. This was particularly significant because of the exceptionally large and unique iron smelting furnaces as well as working areas, buildings and a cemetery all exposed on the line of a new dual carriageway. There was sufficient known about the potential of the site to suggest an evaluation should have been carried out beforehand and perhaps the line of the road changed. It would have justified a large well-resourced excavation and instead we had to make do with a handful of volunteers to learn what we could before the site was destroyed. After the excavation I consoled myself with the knowledge that parts of the site to the east had not been destroyed and could be Scheduled in the future to protect it from further damage. However, I was later told that part of the area had been deep ploughed and the remaining part destroyed when extending a fishing lake. A classic case which shows how legislation to protect archaeological sites is only as effective as those charged with implementing it.

On a more personal note, I also regret my decision not to carry out a full excavation of the Iron Age sites at Wollaston. I had carried out an evaluation for Pioneer Aggregates in 1990 ahead of their plans to quarry the area, and this had revealed a dense line of Iron Age sites or small farms strung out along the gravel terrace. I was asked by the company to carry out a full excavation requested by the Curatorial Section of the Archaeology Unit but declined because of the poor working relationship I had with the County Archaeologist. The Contracting Section of the Archaeology Unit eventually won the contract and carried out the work. It is not that I think I could have done this better, but I would have welcomed the chance to study the pottery and the effects of settlement drift on the population at this time. It is disappointing that there is still no published report on the site.

Finally, and if pushed, I might even admit a regret to not acquiring a formal archaeological qualification. Not because this would have affected the work I carried out – because I never once felt that a lack of a university degree was a handicap, as most of the work was practical and a matter of common sense – but because it would have made my work more credible and more acceptable in the eyes of others. The only real difficulty presented by a lack of formal education and training was in the preparation of written reports. Although I would like to think that there was some inherited literary quality in the North-East Northamptonshire air that produced the likes of Clare, Dryden and Fuller, in truth I was indebted to a host of people who helped in the preparation of reports for many of the more important sites I subsequently excavated.

But these regrets are minor grumbles compared to the years of personal reward and satisfaction gained from my archaeological work. And I know that my drift from builder to amateur and then professional archaeologist, was a process that could never happen today; and rightly so, because the archaeological environment was so different then. But then I would like to think it would be equally difficult for anyone today to make a similar contribution to archaeology in the county as I managed to do at that time with the very limited resources we had available.

In addition to whatever I managed to achieve in a professional role, I am also extremely pleased to have played a small part in the development of amateur archaeology in the county. Since the 1970s the Northamptonshire Archaeology

Society and the Upper Nene Archaeological Society have jointly run much of the amateur side of the archaeology in the county and I am proud to have been a member of both. The work carried out by Roy Friendship Taylor and his wife Liz, on a Roman villa site at Piddington, provides a good example of the excellent contribution that has been made by society members to archaeology in the county.

This has not always been easy, however, as much has been expected from anyone prepared to take on the role of Chairman of the Society and/or Editor of the annual journal, *Northamptonshire Archaeology*. During the 1980s, there was a real danger that the NAS would collapse. Tony Brown who had edited the journal for the previous ten years had retired and Brian Dix had taken on the job. Unfortunately, Brian was unable to devote sufficient time due to work commitments and Roy Friendship Taylor kindly agreed to share this responsibility for the short term. When Brian found he could not continue we desperately tried to find another editor with little success. Fortunately, after contacting Northampton College, Dr Liz Musgrove and later her husband Martin Tingle agreed to edit the Journal. Martin became joint Chairman and Editor of the Journal for the next 15 years and the NAS owes him much for his commitment and the contribution he made over this time. Martin has now left the area but with Andy Chapman taking over as Editor of the Journal, we can be sure of maintaining these high standards.

It was inevitable that my archaeological career would change dramatically towards the end of the century, not least because the ironstone quarries closed, which reduced the need for rescue work, but also because it was very much a transitional period in archaeological terms between the 'enthusiastic' professionalism that went before and the 'scientific' professionalism that has since followed. The death knell for the non-academic professional archaeologist was heard; it just took longer than was expected and longer than was probably healthy for all concerned.

Today the archaeological environment is as far removed from that of 30 years ago as that was from the efforts of the antiquarians some 300 years before. The impact of PPG16 and the massive advances made by science and technology now mean that the archaeologists' world is one of desk-based assessments; non-intrusive surveys, satellite imaging and DNA profiling. A sort of CSI:Archaeology. A modern day archaeologist now needs a wireless laptop before a shovel and can probably have a successful career without ever picking up a trowel in anger.

But this is progress; and I genuinely believe it is far better to recognize and embrace the benefits that have been achieved in this new world than it is to yearn for a past that has now been lost and will never be replaced. And I am constantly reminded of this when I sit at my laptop and marvel at the wonder of Google Earth revealing crop marks and archaeological sites across fields and areas of the county I thought I knew so well.

But elements of the past remain. Perversely, part of the modern day popularisation of archaeology has been achieved by recreating some of the supposed excitement of the rescue years by investigating sites 'just in time', or in this case, within the artificial time limits set by the broadcasters, ..."*and we have just three days to find out*". If only Time Team had been around forty years earlier, we could all have enjoyed the thrill of real rescue archaeology as sites were excavated and destroyed in real time in front of our very eyes. But perhaps not.

CHAPTER EIGHT

Reflections on Iron Age Excavations in the County

During the 25 years that I was a full time professional archaeologist, approximately three-quarters of my time was spent excavating sites of Iron Age date or with origins in that period. Whilst not detracting from the singular significance of sites that were excavated in other periods – especially the Roman Bridge at Aldwincle, iron furnaces at Laxton, and Anglo-Saxon cemetery at Wakerley – it is this aggregated experience of Iron Age sites that encourages me to offer some reflections on these excavations that will hopefully assist others to enhance our overall understanding of life during this time.

I should point out that this is not an attempt to provide a comprehensive account of the Iron Age in Northamptonshire; this has already been done more than adequately by others. More recently, the work carried out as part of the National Mapping Project[27] has expanded the archaeological record of activity during the Iron Age considerably. Instead, this is an attempt to reflect on some of the lessons we learnt and the problems experienced in excavating and interpreting Iron Age sites in the county

I have tried to organise my thoughts under a number of broad headings. But in doing this, it only brings home how interrelated many of these issues are and how difficult it is to compartmentalize any one aspect of Iron Age life without considering the wider implications on other aspects of society at that time. I have nevertheless persevered with this approach using the following broad heading:

- Population and settlement

- Hillforts and other defended enclosures

- Roundhouses and other structures

- Pits and pit alignments

- Agriculture and economy

Population and Settlement

One of the main challenges facing the student of Iron Age archaeology is determining settlement patterns and the density and distribution of the population during this time. There is likely to have been a substantial increase in population over the 700 year lifespan of the period, due in part to advances in agricultural practices and techniques and the introduction of new crops capable of supporting greater numbers of people.

Any population estimates are, of course, heavily influenced by known settlement patterns recorded within the archaeological record. When we excavated a number of Iron Age pits at Upton in 1965, it was only the third time that a settlement site of this period had been excavated in the county. Since that time, numerous excavations have been carried out within the county ranging from full scale excavations to rescue work and trial trenching. Along with the results of fieldwalking and other surveys, especially aerial photography, this has led to a massive increase in the number of known Iron Age sites in the county.

At present, it is estimated that there are around 700 recorded locations of Iron Age activity in Northamptonshire. This suggests an average of around two or three sites or possible settlements per modern parish. On the one hand, this might appear to be an over-estimate as all sites are obviously not contemporaneous and there is frequently evidence of settlement drift. On the other hand of course, many sites have probably been destroyed without record and there are likely to be just as many that are still unrecorded. On balance therefore – and deploying the well-used swings and roundabouts methodology – a figure of this scale may not be entirely unrealistic for any given time during this period. An estimated population of say, 5,000–7,000 or so may not therefore be unreasonable for the mid-late Iron Age period in the county

It is, however, difficult to reliably define and characterize settlement types because only part of a site may ever be exposed and/or excavated and also because it is often difficult to know which features are contemporary. Very often there is no stratigraphical link between houses and other features on a site and dating has to depend on pottery or radiocarbon dating. This is rarely capable of providing sufficient accuracy for shorter time periods, nor for accounting for settlement drift and seasonal occupation (although environmental analysis is of course being increasingly used for this). Even where sites have been fully excavated, it is possible that only one or two phases of a long lived settlement will have been recorded, with further activity extending beyond the range of the excavation.

Moreover earlier phases are often harder to identify, especially if they do not have enclosure ditches and/or have a less distinctive fill with less darkened material than found in later features. Settlements with ditches and enclosures become much more common towards the later part of the period. They are often rectangular in shape and frequently contain between one and three house sites, which may, or may not be contemporary.

In discussing the nature of settlement sites, excavation has also produced examples of open as well as enclosed sites, although on many sites part of the settlement could be open and other parts enclosed. Likewise, it is possible that a settlement was open during an early phase and enclosed later. There are also a number of sites in the county where the main settlement was not enclosed by a ditch but may have had fences or other temporary barriers that have never been located.

Although there is likely to have been variation in settlement patterns due to differing soil types and other environmental factors - with less activity on the heavy soils and more where the land is lighter and more fertile - recent work suggests that this variation may be less marked than was originally thought. For example, the idea that Iron Age settlement is rare on the heavy boulder clays which cover much of the county has been shown to be incorrect. Dick Hollowell recorded numerous sites of this period on the clay geology in the Cogenhoe-Yardley Hastings area and recent development at nearby Milton Keynes has revealed Iron Age sites on the boulder clay at a rate of virtually one every kilometre. At Brigstock, we partially excavated an extensive site on boulder clay that had originated in the early/middle Iron Age and similar features of this period were also excavated on sticky boulder clay at Oakley near Corby.

Conversely, aerial photography has revealed a high density of sites along the fertile Nene Valley, but evidence from excavation has highlighted the extent to which these patterns may represent the result of shifting population, settlement drift and seasonal occupation, rather than the remains of individual and discrete sites.

It is also possible that other environmental factors – in addition to soil type – played a key role in influencing the location of settlements and the distribution of the population. For example, having a convenient water supply and sighting a house on the sunny side of a tall hedge or sheltered by nearby woodland would have been as important considerations. There are a number of settlements in the county where alignments of unenclosed ring gullies or house sites are known and where it is possible they were all sheltered by a large hedge or woodland that has left little trace in the archaeological record. A good example of this is at Long Dole, Crick, where the inhabitants kept rebuilding their houses on the same narrow strip of land that presumably had some protection from the elements. At Wakerley, we found a post hole alignment along the most exposed side of the site, which presumably supported a stockade and gave some protection against the prevailing weather.

Trying to estimate the likely Iron Age population at any one time, is further complicated by the plateau in the calibration curve during this period – which makes radiocarbon dating less sensitive at this time – and by the lack of variation in ceramic assemblages, which also makes accurate dating more difficult. It is for this reason that I have attempted to date the known assemblages more closely and place the excavated sites in a chronological framework based on radiocarbon dates and typologies (see Appendix 1).

Hillforts and Other Defended Enclosures

The most distinctive and iconic representation of settlement during this period remains the ubiquitous hillfort. Although Northamptonshire may not appear to be as well endowed with hillforts as some other counties – certainly not in terms of popular recognition and physical presence in the landscape – there

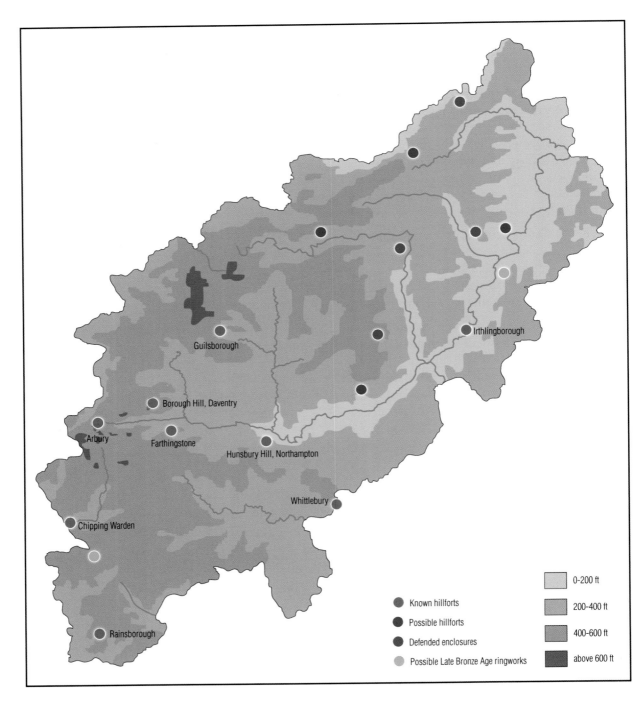

Known hillforts
Possible hillforts
Defended enclosures
Possible Late Bronze Age ringworks

0-200 ft
200-400 ft
400-600 ft
above 600 ft

Guilsborough

Irthlingborough

Borough Hill, Daventry

Arbury

Farthingstone

Hunsbury Hill, Northampton

Whittlebury

Chipping Warden

Rainsborough

8.1 Known and possible hillforts and other defended enclosures in Northamptonshire.

are a number of important sites in the county which suggests that the hillfort was a dominating influence in the area at some time during this period. It is also likely that there are many other hillfort sites in the county that have not survived the centuries of intensive ploughing and other erosion from the Roman period onwards.

A notable feature of the known sites is the equal spacing between locations. There is a line of five probable forts along the west side of the county; Chipping Warden (Arbury Camp), Daventry, (Borough Hill), Guilsborough, Desborough and Gretton (Harborough Farm) which are all around 15kms apart, and a further four forts in the south of the county; Rainsborough, Whittlebury, Farthingstone and Hunsbury with similar spacing. Unfortunately, the position of the possible sites at Desborough and Gretton cannot be proved because the sites have been destroyed by quarrying. They have not been recorded as hillforts, but the locality of Desborough, supported by the finds from the area (e.g. the Desborough mirror), and the direct alignment and spacing of sites at Guilsborough, Desborough and Gretton provides strong support for this hypothesis.

There may also be a line of forts on the east of the county, roughly following the Nene Valley, but only two locations are known at present; Hunsbury and Irthlingborough. There may however have been a site in the Earls Barton/Great Doddington area and the earthwork behind Earls Barton church cannot be excluded as a possible hillfort site. To the north-east beyond Irthlingborough there is strong possibility that there was a fort in the Sudborough parish, or perhaps the earthwork at Wadenhoe, which is on a spur overlooking the River Nene, may have been of this date. Both Sudborough and Wadenhoe are roughly 15kms north of Irthingbrough and a similar distance from Gretton to the north.

Despite their perceived prominence in the landscape, new hillfort sites are still being discovered. For example, Irthlingborough was not discovered until 1984 and Whittlebury in 2006. Part of the village at Whittlebury is built around the fort, whereas most of the other known forts in the county, apart from Guilsborough are situated away from modern villages. The discovery of Irthlingborough and Whittlebury conforms with the pattern of hillfort sites being located at places which include the names 'borough' or 'bury', which supports the suggestion that there may be other sites still to be discovered (e.g. Sudborough).

The known hillforts vary in size from the huge contour fort at Borough Hill, extending over 54 hectares, to the relatively small fort at Hunsbury, covering only 1.6 hectares. Although none of the forts are situated on low ground only the fort at Borough Hill can be said to be defensible on all sides.

Radiocarbon dates from Hunsbury and Rainsborough suggest that they were built between the 8th-5th centuries BC and a small amount of pottery from Irthlingborough and Guilsborough suggest that these also originated in the early Iron Age. If this is the case – and if the suggested spacing is meaningful – then the hillforts could have formed part of a planned landscape at that time.

There has been little examination of hillfort interiors in the county, although the defences have been sectioned on a number of sites. At Rainsborough stone built guard chambers were found flanking the entranceway and stone was also used to revet the rampart. At Hunsbury, excavation revealed that the rampart was a timber-laced box structure in the first phase which was supported at the rear by a stout stockade. This rampart was eventually burnt down in an intense fire, and a recent magnetometer survey has confirmed that this burning continued right around the rampart. Recent trial trenching at Hunsbury has confirmed the presence of an outer ditch around parts of the circuit.

When the interior of the hillfort at Hunsbury was quarried in the late 19th century a local antiquarian estimated there were around 300 pits within the fort and the many finds, now in Northampton museum, support the suggestion that there was extensive activity within the site. Similarly, at Whittlebury a geophysical survey has revealed a concentration of circular structures aligned along the inside of the rampart, and at Borough Hill trial trenching has also suggested widespread and intense activity within the interior of the fort. This site may have originated in the late Bronze Age as a number of tools from this period have been found on the hilltop.

At a later date, a smaller hillfort was built at the northern end of the contour fort at Borough Hill, but nothing is known about the interior apart from the later siting of a Roman villa within the defences. At the recently discovered hillfort at Irthlingborough aerial photographs have revealed evidence of internal features and pottery from the surface suggests a wide date range for the site. Little is known about activity within any of the other hillforts in the county.

Hillforts are commonly viewed as the sites with the highest status during this period. Clearly they would have been an important part of the landscape and would probably have enjoyed a higher status than many other settlement sites, not least because the effort required to construct the ramparts would have required considerable organisation and manpower. But whether or not this proves they were the home of local nobility or tribal chieftains and therefore had a higher status than settlement elsewhere remains uncertain.

There are, for example, other sites in the county where the finds, especially pottery, suggest a degree of prosperity, equal to, if not greater than many hillforts. A good example is the site at Weekley, where defended enclosures, high class pottery and imported goods suggest a site of above average status.

At both Hunsbury and Borough Hill, and also possibly at Rainsborough, satellite enclosures have been located on the hill slopes outside the defences which may have served as outposts to the main sites. At Hunsbury an enclosure was excavated at Wootton Hill Farm, 1km to the south south-west of the hillfort. This was roughly square, approximately 50 metres in diameter, with a deep ditch and evidence of a gateway and possible supports for a stockade in the entrance. The entrance is on the west side which is unusual for an Iron Age enclosure, and this meant that the entrance faced the hillfort. Internally a building was sited beside the entrance which could have been a guard house, and there was a possible lookout tower located in the corner of the enclosure.

Another enclosure was found in a similar position on the north north-west side of the hillfort which may have served a similar purpose. Trial trenching ahead of development confirmed it was a deep ditch of Iron Age date. The enclosure was also square, as at Wootton Hill, but it was double ditched and enclosed a bigger area. It had an entrance on the east side.

An enclosure which may also have been an outpost was located by aerial photography 230m south-east of the hillfort at Borough Hill. The enclosure was broadly the same size and shape as Wootton Hill Farm and the entrance appears to face north-west in the direction of the hillfort. Trial trenching has shown that the enclosure ditch was 3 metres deep but no dating evidence was found

The siting of both the possible satellite enclosures at Hunsbury and Borough Hill would have given the inhabitants of the hillsforts a much better view of the surrounding landscapes, especially if lookout towers were included within them. In the 1960s there were at least twenty other sites in the country where a possible satellite enclosure is recorded near a hillfort. This suggests there is still plenty of work to do to fully understand the role and function of hillforts; their place within the landscape, and their relationship with other communities and settlements within Iron Age society.

Hillforts are of course, just one form of defended enclosure. Along with the hill top at Borough Hill, which was almost certainly occupied in the late Bronze Age, the other earliest example of a defended enclosure is the Ringwork at Thrapston which was radiocarbon dated to the 9th-6th centuries BC. This was partially excavated in 2002 and the ceramic assemblage supports this date. The only other example in the county is at Thenford in the south and although no excavation has taken place to date the site, a late Bronze Age hoard and other finds have been found in the vicinity of the earthwork. Ringworks are rare in the Midlands, but where investigated elsewhere they appear to have had a defensive function.

Defended enclosures become much more common during the latter half of the Iron Age and a number of important sites of this type have been excavated in the county. These include the sites at Aldwincle, Twywell, Wakerley, Weekley and Stanwell Spinney, Wellingborough. In 1986, another similar site was excavated on a housing development at Wootton Hill Farm close to Hunsbury hillfort (referred to above). It proved to have the same distinctive style to the previously excavated sites and has since become the type site for what is now known as the Wootton Hill Farm type settlement (WHF) (see Figure 6.6, page 100).

All of these sites are rectangular defended enclosures with deeper ditches than average and with post holes and trenches in their entrances that would have supported gateways and stockades. Most of these sites are situated on higher ground with the exception of the enclosure at Aldwincle which lies in the Nene Valley. It was however situated alongside Harpers Brook which may have acted as an extra line of defence on one side.

In each case the gateway trenches were inset from the entrance and presumably supported the end of a stockade which continued along the top of the bank.

The gateways themselves between the stockade were around 2 metres wide on average and it is assumed the end posts in the stockade supported a gate structure. Post pits between the stockade and the ditch at Wootton Hill Farm and a slot in a similar position at Aldwincle suggests that in some entrances at least the end of the bank was retained in a box like structure built of timber or turf.

With some entranceways, the plan is complicated by rebuilding. For instance, the flat stone slabs at Wootton Hill Farm seem likely to have served as post pads in a rebuilding phase, which may also be the case with the stonework at Aldwincle. Similarly, the arrangement of trenches and post pits in the entrance to Enclosure C at Weekley (see Figures 5.17 and 5.18, pages 84–85) may also be confused by successive periods of rebuilding. The stockade trench is no more than 0.5 metres from the edge of the ditch and the whole arrangement gives the impression that the gateway was sited between the ditch ends. However, the ditch is some 6.5 metres wide at this point and a possible re-cutting of the ditch on the inside as well as erosion on the edges is probably creating a misleading picture. If the first phase of the ditch was centred further to the east, the position of the stockade trenches and post pits would be comparable to elsewhere. The ditch was over 3 metres deep at this point and the bottom rested on a seam of estuarine limestone which had been partially removed. Perhaps obtaining the stone was the reason for the recutting.

The width of gateways between the stockade trenches was fairly consistent in each of the WHF sites, averaging about 2 metres at most sites. There was more variation in the width of the causeway between the ditch ends, which varied from 3 metres at Wootton Hill farm to 11.5 metres at Wakerley (Enclosure A).

The ceramic evidence suggests that WHF type enclosures all date to the 2nd-1st centuries BC, with two later sites (Weekley and Wakerley, Enclosure A) dating to the 1st century AD. This was probably a period of change and uncertainty and the strengthening of the defences may have been designed as additional protection against a potential enemy and/or a display of power and prestige for similar ends. The defences all seem unnecessarily strong if only designed for animal control and/or to prevent rustling etc.

In addition, there are a number of other enclosures in the county that may be a similar type which have deep ditches but where the entranceways have not been excavated. These included the possible outpost on the north side of Hunsbury hillfort; the satellite enclosure to the south east of Borough Hill, Daventry and a site at Great Doddington. Similarly, there are two other small enclosures – at Brigstock and Draughton – which both have larger defences than might reasonably be expected.

Despite the difficulties in defining the limits of Iron Age settlements (discussed above), I am confident that the plans of two large Iron Age sites excavated in the county – at Wakerley (see Figures 5.1 and 5.2, pages 72–73) and Weekley (see Figure 5.17, page 84) – were reasonably complete, even though there may still have been earlier activity outside of the excavated areas. At Wakerley, the boundaries of the settlement were clearly identified on three sides, but the area to the north-west was not exposed and as an earlier pit was located near this side of the settlement, there may have been an earlier phase extending towards the north-west. The type of settlement revealed by the plan suggests that an area was enclosed by a deep ditch around the 2nd century BC which may have been designed to constrain stock movements. The houses at this time were situated to the north-west of this enclosure and may have initially have been unenclosed. The houses were eventually enclosed by a deep ditch, probably in the early 1st century AD.

At Weekley, a number of small Iron Age enclosures were superseded by two enclosures with very deep ditches and a defended gateway by the end of the period. There were few obvious house sites within the enclosures and it is possible they were located on the pervious soil to the east in an area destroyed by quarrying. By coincidence we located a house site some 100 metres west of the main enclosures situated between two trackway ditches. Large amounts of decorated ware were found in the ditches adjacent to the house site and it has been suggested that this may have been a guard house at the approaches to the settlement.

Two recent excavations in the county – at Crick and Courtenhall – have revealed unusual plans. At Crick, a large number of ring gullies were exposed over a big area, with few of them enclosed by ditches. Not all the gullies may have been house sites, but the large number of potential houses may indicate settlement drift and/or seasonal use over a period of time.

At Courtenhall, five clusters of Iron Age and Roman features were excavated after a large area was cleared of topsoil prior to housing development. Three of these sites, or areas of activity, were spaced some 3-400 metres apart, and appear to have originated in the middle Iron Age. Based on the ceramic evidence the three sites appear to have been in use at the same time, probably between 250 and 50BC. The other two clusters represent settlement drift and date to the late Iron Age and Roman periods. The earliest diagnostic pottery found during the excavation, dated to around the 4th century BC, came from two pits located on the east side of the area, suggesting that occupation may have began in this area. Interestingly, another cluster of features has been exposed by aerial photography, nearby but just outside the area of excavation.

The three middle Iron Age sites at Courtenhall varied in character and illustrate the diversity of activity on some Iron Age settlements. In one area at least three house sites, within drainage gullies, were located and although the total area of settlement was not revealed, they appeared to be unenclosed. In another area, two small enclosures overlying an earlier track were recovered and a group of some 40 pits were situated around the outside of one of the enclosures.

In summary, excavation has shown that it is not easy to define the type and size of Iron Age settlements unless boundaries are clearly revealed, or can be implied with confidence. Some settlements appear to have been occupied for hundreds of years, perhaps with people drifting around a limited area over that time, possibly changing the type and nature of land use according to circumstances. Although ditches are increasingly used towards the later part of the period – either for drainage or to provide enclosure – this is not always the case and later settlements with no obvious enclosure are still found.

But the existence of a significant number of defended enclosures – including hillforts in the early to middle part of the period and Wootton Hill type settlements in the latter half – supports the notion of a highly populated and partly planned landscape over much of this time. The possible existence of satellite enclosures associated with hillfort sites provides further evidence of a planned landscape integrating settlements of differing types and functions. This again suggests the need for further work to better understand the nature and role of different settlement types and their interrelationships during this period.

Roundhouses and Other Structures

Although most enclosures are assumed to be the site of habitation – and there are some that are clearly not – it is the familiar presence of the roundhouse or hut that usually provides conclusive evidence of human occupation. Numerous Iron Age house sites have now been excavated in the county and there is a good wealth of knowledge of the different types of hut design and construction that may have been in use during the period.

8.2 Plan of Iron Age roundhouse at Brigstock.

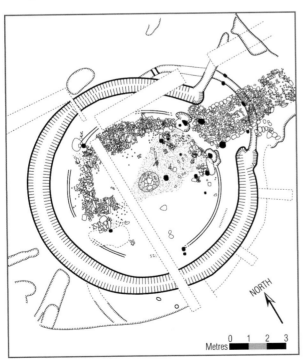

Metres 0 1 2 3

NORTH

In many cases, the surviving plan often consists of little more than the surrounding drainage gully and occasionally the post holes for the doorway. The need for a gully often depends on the geology, although they occur more often on later Iron Age sites. The door posts and the wall line are usually inset from the drainage gully and presumably the eaves of the house extended to the gully. Rubbish and other remains including pot sherds, are often found in the gullies during excavation, which often provide key dating evidence. Houses without drainage gullies are more difficult to locate, either by aerial photography or geophysical survey and, where found, can be equally difficult to date, without the evidence of material collected in the gully.

There are however three house sites in Northamptonshire – at Brigstock, Wakerley and Aldwincle – where more structural detail has survived that warrants further description. Brigstock provided a good example of a house with a clearly defined gully. Here the house had been built within a small enclosure and the surviving bank had protected the internal features from plough damage. The position of the house wall was defined by a shallow slot which would not have survived in an area that had been ploughed. The doorway post holes were substantial and would have survived. The house wall would presumably have been constructed with wattle work, perhaps supported by turf or clay. The house itself was 7.8 metres in diameter with a distance of 1.4 metres from the wall line to the centre of the drainage gully.

Crushed chalk, presumably retrieved from the boulder clay bank enclosure, was found within the house and may have been used as flooring. Limestone slabs were also found on the house floor close to the wall trench. The stone path leading to the house was largely comprised of glacial pebbles which would also have been extracted from the boulder clay. The use of stone on Iron Age sites is unusual within the Northamptonshire area. Trial trenching carried out by Pat Foster has shown that stonework was also used in other nearby features and was not confined to the one house.

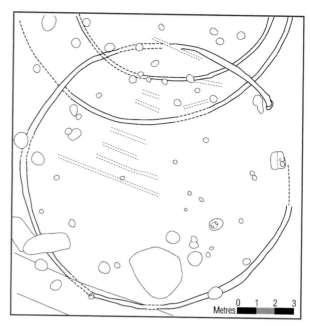

8.3 Plan of Iron Age roundhouse at Wakerley.

Houses without drainage gullies are much less common from the middle Iron Age onwards but do still occur on well drained sites, such as that excavated at Wakerley. With this type of house the wall is set in a bedding trench and was presumably constructed with stakes and wattle work. The post holes at the entrance were elongated and there may have been two posts on either side of the doorway. The main thrust of the roof is taken by a ring beam supported by an inner ring of posts. There were six houses of this type excavated at Wakerley, but some were replacements and there would have been no more than three in use at any one time. The houses ranged from 8-14 metres in diameter and each was built to the same design. The two largest, both with a diameter of 14 metres, were exceptionally large for Iron Age houses.

8.4 Plan of Iron Age roundhouse at Aldwincle.

The house excavated at Aldwincle was notable for the amount of structural detail it provided. The site was situated on low lying ground with a bedrock of glacial silt and was probably poorly drained. During the final phase of the house it had been burnt down and the individual stake holes in the house wall could clearly be identified by the charcoal filling.

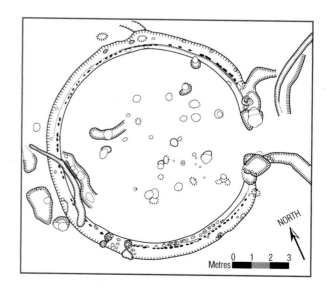

The wall consisted of split timbers, between 9-18cm in diameter and with the flat side of the post set against the inner edge of the trench. They were set close together but were presumably linked together by wattle work. A total of 132 upright timbers were used in the wall, with a further ring of 24 posts set 38cm outside the wall which may have held posts supporting the ends of the rafters.

This house was 11 metres in diameter with a doorway at least 1.5 metres wide positioned on the east side. There was a second doorway about 1 metre wide situated on the south-west side of the house in the second phase of the building. Internally there were a number of post holes situated midway between the outer wall and the centre of the house, which may have held posts supporting the roof or forming partitions. The house site had been badly truncated by medieval ploughing and it was fortunate that so much detail had survived.

Circular buildings may have been used for a variety of purposes, but it is presumed that most were house sites, in the absence of evidence to the contrary. Likewise, buildings raised above the ground on four stout posts are usually presumed to be granaries but this may not always have been the case. Some four-post structures may have supported platforms for exposing the dead and others may have supported lookout towers. The square structures recorded in the corners of defensive enclosures at Wootton Hill Farm, Weekley and Wakerley were almost certainly look-out towers. The structure at Wakerley was particularly unusual; here a four-post structure had been replaced by a large six -post arrangement incorporated within a circular structure.

On sites that have been intensively occupied over a prolonged period of time, such as Weekley and Wakerley, it is common to find hundreds of post holes spread across the site. They may have had a variety of uses including fence lines, supporting small sheds and drying racks. Some of these small structures have drainage gullies around them to keep them dry and can easily be mistaken for house sites.

Pits and Pit Alignments

If the hillfort represents the iconic image of the Iron Age period above ground then the same can probably said for the humble pit below ground. The majority of Iron Age sites have involved the identification and subsequent excavation of pits of varying shapes, most of which would have been used for storage. The number of pits revealed varies considerably between similar WHF sites, which may suggest changing practices over time and/or varied need depending on settlement size, geology, agricultural practices etc.

The settlement site at Twywell revealed an unusually large number of pits. These were located in two distinct groups with 90 pits recorded within the enclosure and a further 87 lying outside the enclosure ditch. It is clear from the plan that a number of pits towards the east had been destroyed before the site was excavated and so a figure of well over 200 seems more likely. In comparison, at the large excavations at Wakerley and Weekley, there were only 26 and 32 pits recorded respectively and only 24 and 6 at the other WHF type sites at Aldwincle and Wootton Hill Farm. The only other site in the county where a large number of pits may have existed is the hillfort at Hunsbury where antiquarians estimated that over 300 pits were destroyed during quarrying. It seems that the use of pits – for whatever purpose – was at its height during the 4th-2nd centuries BC as proportionately less are found on later sites.

It has been suggested that storage pits could only be used where the underlying geology was dry which explains the variation in usage between sites. However, no pits were found on sites at Crick and Grendon where the geology was suitable and at Aldwincle there was a spring draining water onto the site and if the same conditions occurred in the Iron Age the enclosure ditch would have kept the inner area dry and hence suitable for storage.

The large number of pits at Twywell were presumably used for the storage of agricultural products, which was supported by the grain residue found within a pit. However, the group of pits within the enclosure – dating to between the mid 4th- mid 3rd centuries BC – also included a number of animal and human burials which might suggest a more ritualistic function. There was no evidence of any similar activity in the later pits located outside the enclosure, although the bones of five dogs was an unusual find in one pit. If it is assumed that the inhabitants were not eating the dogs, then they must have been dumped in the pit when they died – either over a period of time or due to a common disease or attack.

On later sites where there are few if any pits recorded, an alternative method of storage must have been used, either granaries raised above the ground or perhaps the use of some form of central storage facility away from what would have been sites occupied for seasonal agricultural use only.

Although single pits, or complexes of pits, have a fairly well-understood functional role, the purpose of pits constructed in a linear pattern, or alignment, remains far more enigmatic. Part of the difficulty in interpreting these features is caused by the fact that many alignments have been dug on a regular pattern and consist of pits of similar size, shape and spacing. Excavation has also revealed that many pits have a similar profile, usually consisting of steep sides, angled corners and a flat-bottom.

Excavation of many pit alignments, both within the county and elsewhere, has failed to find conclusive proof of the role of these features. Although they are commonly interpreted as land boundaries, this does not explain why they were constructed on such a regular pattern and with such obvious care. Based on my experience of excavating pits in eight alignments on six different sites in the county, I have recently developed a theory which might explain their nature and purpose. This is discussed in the following chapter.

Agriculture and Economy

Iron Age farmers would have practiced both arable farming and animal husbandry, but it is uncertain whether agriculture was carried out on a community basis or whether individual settlements or households catered for themselves. A study of the animal bones found on Iron Age sites in the county shows that cattle, sheep and goats were common, with slightly more sheep present than cattle. Wheat and barley were the most common crops grown.

The proportion of land used for arable, pasture and woodland remains uncertain, but it is likely that as today there would be more land farmed on the lighter soils and in the river valleys and more woodland remaining on the heavier and less productive soils. Pollen analysis has shown that most of the vegetation existing today, including weeds, would have been in existence during the Iron Age.

Keeping a supply of grain, either for consumption, or as seed corn, would have been an important requirement for Iron Age settlements. Excavation has shown that various methods were used to store and preserve grain. In the early part of the period, granaries raised above the ground seem to have been preferred but by the middle Iron Age storage in pits was becoming more common (see above).

Quern stones for grinding corn have been found on a number of Iron Age sites and the large collection from the hillfort at Hunsbury suggests they were trade items, brought to the site from locations elsewhere, along with other agricultural tools such as plough shares etc. The existence of trackways between major settlements becomes more common during the later part of the period and these would have become increasingly important trade routes as the economy developed.

The ironstone outcrop that runs across Northamptonshire has made the area a popular location for iron working, especially in the north-east part of the county. There is widespread evidence of iron working in most parishes between Corby and Stamford, and although much of this is dated to the Romano-British period, there is evidence of earlier activity in a number of sites during the Iron Age.

One of the earliest possible sites of iron working was found at Great Oakley just outside Corby. The remains of a bowl furnace was found on a quarry site which could date to the late Bronze Age-early Iron Age period, and if so, would make this one of the earliest known sites of this type in the country. Nearby at Bulwick, we discovered the site of five surface shaft furnaces and 19 channel hearths filled with black ashy soil at the surface level. A number of pits were also found on the site and a section in the quarry face showed that they had obviously been dug to extract nodular ironstone. The pits were dug through a layer of estuarine clay which could have been used in the construction of the furnaces. Similar furnace remains were found in the nearby parish of Gretton

Dating evidence for the site at Bulwick was ambiguous but furnaces of this type are known from the Roman period.

In the same area we found abundant evidence of iron working on the large Iron Age and Romano-British site at Wakerley. Three types of furnace were identified: the bowl furnace; the sunken shaft furnace and the surface shaft furnace. Of these, the sunken shaft furnace – with the shaft built in a pit with no provision for tapping the slag – was most unusual, if not unique. Dating evidence was sparse but there are likely to date to between the 1st century BC and 1st century AD. Two of these furnaces were lifted and taken to the Natural History Museum in London.

Further evidence of possible iron working during the Iron Age was found at Hunsbury, where the hillfort sits on the southern outcrop of ironstone. Large conglomerates of slag have been found in the ramparts and a large number of unfinished iron tools were apparently discovered during quarrying earlier in the century. It is possible, however, that the slag was formed during an intensive fire when the settlement burnt down and it does seem unlikely that the inhabitants would position their furnaces close to the defences because of the fire risk. This possibility is supported by the slag and Iron Age pottery found in a number of irregular shaped pits outside the fort which appear to have been dug as quarries as the inhabitants searched for better quality stone.

Any discussion of past iron working in the county must make mention of Laxton – albeit with most recorded activity being during the Roman period. Iron working here appears to have been carried out on a massive scale with furnace debris filling the valley floor to an area of around 100 metres wide by 2 metres deep. The existence of nearby buildings and a cemetery support the idea of a substantial industrial complex, and the use of bricks in the construction of the furnaces – more usual in pottery kilns – suggests there may have been a connection between pottery manufacture and iron working in the area. Interestingly, a stretch of Roman road in the Kings Cliffe area is aligned on Laxton and the famous pottery producing area of Caster. The scale of iron working at Laxton certainly raises questions about the organization and control of this activity, which may have had military involvement. It also raises unanswered questions about when iron working started in the area.

Despite such large furnaces being virtually unknown in Britain, by a strange coincidence the remains of a furnace of similar size was revealed by roadworks at Byfield in the south of the county in the same year. However, the furnace which showed evidence of being re-used on a number of occasions, was poorly preserved, and no further evidence of activity was recorded.

For the Future

In this chapter, I have tried to provide some personal reflections on what I think we have learned from Iron Age excavations in the county over the past 40 years. If nothing else, it has provided a healthy reminder of the progress that has been made in our knowledge and understanding over this time. Perhaps more worryingly, it also reminds us that we may look back in another forty years and view our current level of knoweldge with the same degree of naivety that we now view the 1960s. But I guess this is the price of progress.

There should certainly be significant advances in our understanding of the period in the years to come, not least because the results from three major excavations – at Crick, Stanwick and Wollaston – have yet to be published. Each of these sites are different and the combined effect of their publication should throw important new light on the nature of Iron Age settlement and activity in the area. It must however be a matter of regret, that this work, carried out in the 1980s and 90s, remains unpublished. There should surely be a mechanism to ensure that contractors publish excavation results within a reasonable time period.

In terms of priorities for the future, I think it is vitally important that we continue to refine the dating of pottery from Iron Age sites in the region and to ensure the maximum benefits are obtained from advances in scientific dating methods. Without more accurate and consistent dating it will remain difficult to understand the contemporaneity of settlement patterns during the period and questions of population size and distribution and the relationships between different settlement types will remain unanswered.

A lot is now known about the late Iron Age and early Roman sites in the county, and future priority should therefore be given to early Iron Age sites. Although survival is often poor on sites of this period, the excavations at Borough Hill and Weekley Hall Wood show that features can survive under the right conditions and with careful excavation.

I have included my views on the scope for further research on pit alignments in the following chapter. I think there is also scope for further work on iron working in the county, based on the importance of sites already known such as Laxton. With quarrying unlikely to expose sites as in the past, it may be necessary to identify possible furnace sites through fieldwalking to collect slag from the surface of Iron Age sites.

And finally, in these days of strategies and research objectives, it seems appropriate to conclude with the type of questions that future work on the Iron Age in the county might hopefully address. In the interests of brevity, I have restricted myself to just six questions:

i) Are population estimates reasonable when considering the effects of settlement drift and seasonal occupation?

ii) Is there a genuine increase in the number of settlements from the middle Iron Age onwards or are earlier settlements just more difficult to identify?

iii) Can hierarchy and status be recognised within the archaeological record and is defensive capability a good measure of wealth and power?

iv) To what extent are settlement patterns influenced by geological and environmental conditions or is any variation merely a result of differing rates of survival and recording within the archaeological record?

v) What is the relationship between hillforts and other forms of settlement during the period and how does this change over time?

vi) What was the function of pit alignments and how do these features relate to other boundaries within the prehistoric landscape? How, and in what way, did these inter-relationships change over time?

CHAPTER NINE

Pit Alignments – A New Theory

Pit alignments remain one of the most enigmatic features of the prehistoric landscape. While single pits – or pit complexes – and the linear ditch all have a fairly well-understood purpose, the function of pits constructed in an alignment is still shrouded in mystery. Excavation and survey of many pit alignments, both within the county and elsewhere, has failed to find conclusive proof of the role of these features. In the absence of an agreed function, commentators have ascribed a range of less tangible roles to pit alignments, with the most common suggestions being boundaries (with obvious gaps) and symbolic and ritual markers within the landscape.

During my career, I excavated pits in eight alignments on six different sites in the county, including those at Gretton, Briar Hill, Aldwincle, Ringstead and Grendon. This experience, together with the extensive survey work carried out in recent years which has shown that pit alignments are relatively common features within the landscape, has encouraged me to propose a new theory that may explain their nature and purpose. This is discussed below.

Pit Alignments in Northamptonshire

The first pit alignment I excavated was at Briar Hill in 1969. At that time, there were only around 25 known sites in the county, mainly mapped from aerial photography, with very few having been excavated. At the time of writing, it is now estimated (by the National Mapping Programme, NMP), that there are over 140 known alignments in the county covering a total estimated distance of over 35km. As even this figure is likely to underestimate the total – partly due to variations in geology, as discussed below – it is clear that the pit alignment must have represented a common, and presumably an important feature, within the prehistoric landscape.

One of the distinguishing characteristics of pits within an alignment is their uniform shape and positioning. The pits are usually constructed to a regular pattern; with a similar size and shape – mostly rectangular – and often with similar spacing between each one. Of those pits mapped by the NMP, over three-quarters are either oblong or rectangular, with the remainder being unknown or round. The rectangular shaped pits are usually less than 2.5 metres long and 1.8 metres wide with the longer axis always in line with the overall orientation of the alignment. When excavated, they are frequently found to have steep sides with a flat rectangular bottom.

The majority of known alignments in the county occur on permeable geology, particularly the terrace gravels, Northampton Sand and Limestone and Great Oolite Limestone, which may of course reflect the in-built bias in survey

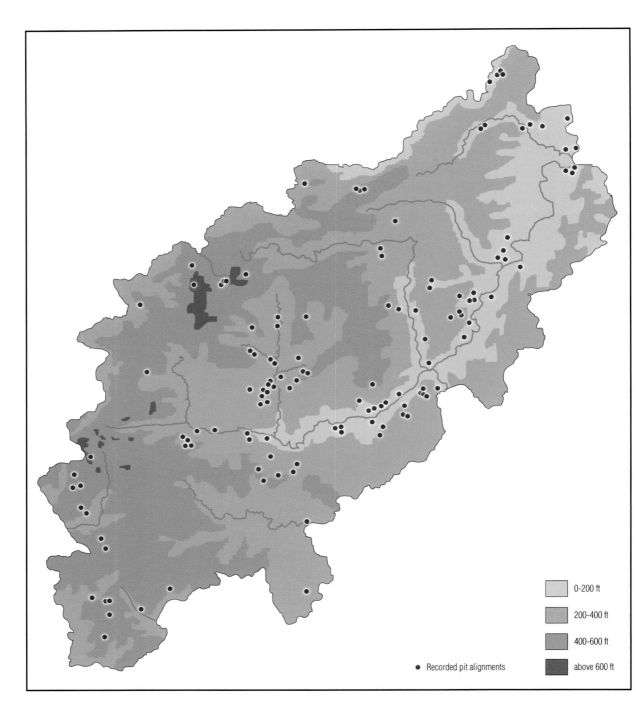

0-200 ft
200-400 ft
400-600 ft
above 600 ft

● Recorded pit alignments

9.1 Known pit alignments in Northamptonshire.

methodology. However, the NMP showed that nearly a quarter of all pit alignments appeared to extend into the less permeable areas, particularly within the Upper Lias Clays, which suggests that there may still be a considerable number of unrecorded features within the county.

In terms of dating, the excavation of all types of pit alignments in England and Wales suggests a wide range extending from the Neolithic to the Roman period. However, alignments with rectangular or oblong shaped pits appear to have a narrower timeframe usually from within the late Bronze Age to middle Iron Age periods. Despite finding early Iron Age pottery in pits at Grendon and Ringstead, it was only recently that radiocarbon dates have been obtained from charcoal and animal bones that date the pits at Grendon and Gayhurst (Buckinghamshire) to a period between the 8th–6th centuries BC. This date is consistent with the pottery and stratigraphy from elsewhere and implies that rectangular pit alignments were in use during a period when most of the hillforts in the county were being constructed.

The Purpose of Pit Alignments

Pit alignments are commonly thought to be boundaries, either between different land holdings to define ownership or as barriers to control stock, perhaps to prevent animals from straying onto arable fields. An alternative view suggests that they may have had a symbolic rather than functional role, perhaps acting as markers in the landscape for various forms of ritual activity, perhaps not unlike 'beating the bounds' carried out in more recent times. Either way, surveys have shown that alignments can extend for considerable distances – and at Grendon I recorded an alignment of 40 pits extending over 500 metres – which supports the view that they fulfilled an important role at the wider community level rather at that of the individual settlement.

The puzzling questions that remain are why these alignments were constructed on such a regular pattern and why individual pits were dug with such care and consistency, especially if they were designed as simple boundaries or barriers. This also leaves aside the rather obvious fact that there would have been some significant gaps if pit alignments were used as barriers, and there is no evidence that the upcast from pits was ever used to re-inforce a barrier, either on either side of an alignment or between the pits.

It is also clear from the pits excavated in firm geology such as the limestone bedrock at Gretton, that considerable efforts were made to provide angled corners and flat bottoms, which is not a particularly easy task, especially when pits were, on average, over a metre deep in solid limestone. (Elsewhere, where pits have been dug into softer sand and gravel, erosion has often affected this square profile). Again, it is questionable why such an effort was made, when the same result might have been more easily achieved by digging pits, or even a continuous ditch, with a traditional sloping or U-shaped profile.

The answer to these questions may lie in examining the role that pit alignments may have played in the evolution of land boundaries during the early Iron Age period and the inter-relationship between such man-made features and other natural barriers such as hedges and water courses. A useful starting point for this is provided by excavations at Briar Hill in the late 1960s.

When we excavated part of a pit alignment at Briar Hill in 1969, we found that the normal shaped pits overlay a number of smaller pits or post holes. These earlier pits were on average 50cm deep and up to 75cm in diameter and there was evidence that they supported posts. The upper edges of the pits appeared to be eroded so if they had held posts they had probably not been backfilled. Some of the pits appeared to be unevenly spaced, but there may have been a double row before some of them were destroyed when the later pits were dug. One possible explanation is that the posts supported a fence, possibly during two phases, although the irregular spacing of the posts and the fact the holes were not back filled casts doubt on this.

An alternative possibility is that the holes supported what is known as a 'dead hedge'. This is a barrier of cut branches and foliage, often interwoven to form a barrier used to enclose or exclude animals from certain parts of the land. It is known from Anglo-Saxon manorial documents that dead hedges were in use before Domesday and they were also commonly used from the start of the Tudor period to control deer, especially from freshly coppiced ground. They were eventually replaced by the barbed wire fence and have since largely gone out of use. As they are not permanent features, dead hedges – like barbed wire fences - are very flexible and can easily be moved or adjusted to meet varying agricultural and pastoral needs.

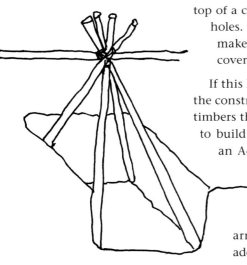

9.2 Example of possible timber 'pyramid' framework supporting a 'dead hedge' in a pit alignment showing the use of a typical rectangular pit profile.

In the case of these early pits, the branches and shrubs could be lashed at the top of a cross frame and there would have been no need to fill the remaining holes. Leaving the holes open would have enabled the farmers to quickly make a passage for animals through the hedge by taking out a section and covering the holes.

If this hypothesis is correct, the same principles could have been applied in the construction of the later pit alignment. If the pits were designed to support timbers this could explain their consistent spacing and shape. The easiest way to build a timber fence in association with the pits would be to construct an A-frame and stand each end in adjacent pits with the apex blocking the space between the two pits. While a single frame may have been sufficient to form a barrier to animals, the width of the pits in the alignment suggests the structure may have been wider, either a double set of A-frames or some form of pyramid arrangement. Other horizontal timbers and hedging may have been added to stop smaller animals getting through.

FACING PAGE
9.3 Examples of possible timber frameworks supporting a 'dead hedge' in pit alignments. (Top three illustrations shown in elevation and bottom two in plan).

As with the dead hedge in the earlier phase, it would have been easy to take out one or two frames and cover the pit or pits to provide access through the barrier at any point along the alignment. This form of barrier would not have stopped people from crossing from one side to the other whilst keeping animals under control. This could have been particularly useful when crops were being rotated in mixed fields. An alignment recently excavated at Raunds was found to follow the boundary between the lighter and heavier soils and the pits – and the suggested 'dead hedge' boundary could have been used to provide temporary, and flexible, separation between the arable and pasture fields.

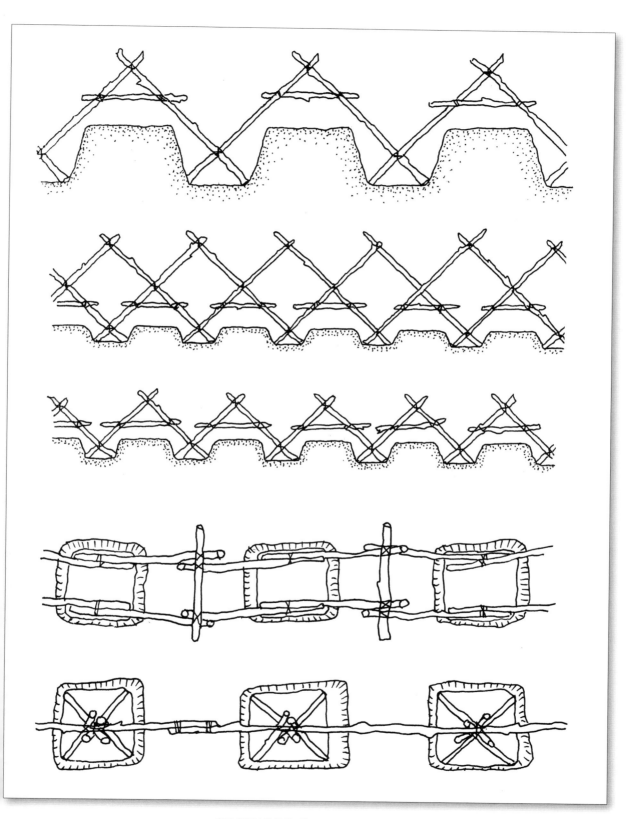

An alternative type of 'dead hedge' has been put forward by Graham Cadman (in correspondence) who suggests that they may have been made out of sheaves or bundles of whatever vegetative material was available locally. This might have included riverside/marsh vegetation, hedgerow and woodland material, waste straw and other products from arable and pastoral fields and other waste vegetation. As such the type and quantity of material used would vary seasonally and by locality. These sheaves or bundles may have been supported by the type of A-frame discussed above, or, in some cases, they have been large enough to be placed directly in the pits themselves, providing an even more flexible barrier perhaps for short-term use

During the excavation of a Neolithic Causewayed Enclosure at Briar Hill in the early 1970s, part of another pit alignment was found close to the earlier one excavated in 1969, this time consisting of large pits that were rounded rather than angular. In 1991 another alignment of smaller rounded pits was excavated at St. Ives in Cambridgeshire and similar features have recently been discovered at Grendon and Gayhurst, Buckinghamshire. At each of these locations the alignments of earlier rounded pits were replaced by the larger rectangular examples.

It is possible, therefore, that there was a gradual evolution in the construction of dead hedge boundaries, starting with a single post arrangement and progressing through the use of small pits of variable sizes and leading to the more common rectangular arrangement, using some form of timber framework to support the hedge. Crucially this hypothesis would provide an explanation for the distinctive spacing and size and shape of rectangular pits. The equal spacing would have been determined by the known size of the A-frame – possibly having been pre-constructed – and the square, steep-sided pits would be the best shape for holding the leg of the frames in position

An alignment excavated at St Ives, Cambridgeshire, provides an interesting example of normal rectangular pits running parallel to the edge of a paleochannel. The filling of the pits had been waterlogged and silted up with alluvial clay. Pieces of wood, mainly thin round wood, up to 6cm in diameter, and hedging debris, mainly blackthorn, oak and field maple, were found in the majority of the pits. A second alignment of smaller round pits followed a similar line approximately 10m to the west and appeared to be earlier in date. The wood found in the pits may have come from a nearby hedge or perhaps from the line of smaller posts which may have supported a timber barrier. Alternatively of course, it may have been debris remaining from the type of dead hedges and timber framework described above.

Ditches were later dug along the line of the pits and continued to be used into the Roman period. If the paleochannel contained water this would have acted as a boundary without the need for other man made boundaries. But the fact that the line was maintained for such a long period of time suggests that it bordered something significant, such as an area of marshland. There may also have been a need to control access at different times of the year according to variable water levels and the type of flexible barrier provided by the proposed pit alignments might have fulfilled this role.

It might be argued that a simple fence would have provided an easier way of containing animals and although alignments of post holes that may have supported a fence or stockade are known, they are not common, perhaps due to the difficulty of detection. It seems certain that simple fences and palisades would also have been in use but they may not have been as robust and as flexible as pits with timber frames, especially over large areas.

It might also be suggested that the use of timber frameworks would have required an excessive amount of timber. For example, it can be estimated that a pit alignment of say 100 metres would have required over 65 poles, each 2.5-3 metres in length, for a single frame and twice this for a double frame. Although this would represent a significant demand, it is likely that timber was plentiful at the time, especially when considering the amount that would have been used in the construction of timber-laced defences at hillforts such as Hunsbury.

If pit alignments were used as flexible boundaries then it is reasonable to assume that they would start or end at other natural features such as hedges or watercourses, or would connect to other man-made barriers such as pits, fences and live or dead hedges. It seems likely that land boundaries would have consisted of all of these different forms, with a combination of features being used according to local circumstances and topography. Pit alignments with a timber framework may have been used where flexibility in access and land use was a particular requirement.

However, few of these other forms of boundary survive sufficiently well within the archaeological record, leaving the more substantial pit alignments to appear isolated within the landscape and not connected in any obvious way to other forms of barrier that might demonstrate their purpose. There is, however, evidence from a number of sites, such as Wollaston and Grendon, that rows of pits were replaced by later ditches in the middle to later Iron Age on similar alignments which suggests a continuity in land boundary usage over a considerable period of time. Such continuity might imply that similar boundary lines may have remained in place over long time periods, possibly evolving from natural features to the various forms of man-made barriers discussed above.

Further evidence of a relationship between pit alignments and other boundary lines was found at Gretton where a row of pits formed a T-junction with a later ditch. It is possible that the ditch was dug to replace an earlier natural feature such as a hedge or line of woodland which may have been co-terminus with the pit alignment. The last pit in the alignment, (F41), was smaller and on the opposite side of the ditch. This could be interpreted as a base for the foot of the last A-frame in line, and it is possible that a nearby feature (F42) was also associated with this arrangement. The fourth pit from the ditch (F37) was slightly off line and a lot shallower. This may have been a convenient place for a gateway or opening between fields with the pit dug at a later stage to plug the gap.

In conclusion, it seems clear that pit alignments were a prominent feature in the early Iron Age landscape. The regularity of their size, shape and spacing and the extra care and effort required for their construction suggests they fulfilled a recognized and important functional role within the community. The use of such a regular pattern or template also suggests an element of control and/or a common understanding of construction requirements that crossed different geo-spatial boundaries.

Moreover, the consistent and distinctive profile of many rectangular pits, revealed by excavation, suggests strongly that they were designed for a specific purpose. This may have been to facilitate the use of timber-frameworks to support a system of dead-hedges which would have provided a prominent and robust barrier that was also highly flexible to meet changing needs almost immediately. These alignments would have been integrated with other forms of natural and man-made barriers, many of which no longer survive, to manage changing land use needs in the best possible way.

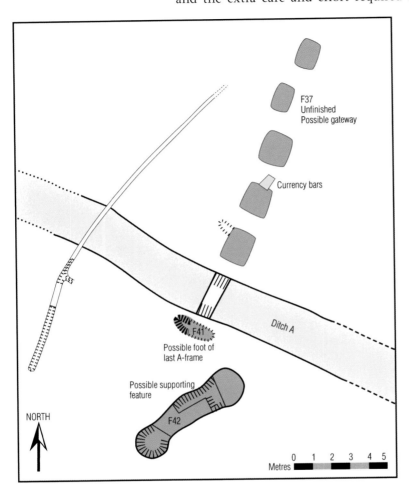

9.4 Pit alignment at Gretton showing possible relationship between pits and later ditch which may have replaced an earlier natural boundry.

F37
Unfinished
Possible gateway

Currency bars

Ditch A

F41
Possible foot of
last A-frame

Possible supporting
feature

F42

NORTH

0 1 2 3 4 5
Metres

APPENDICES

A Proposed Chronology of Iron Age Ceramic Assemblages

This chapter outlines a proposed chronology of late Bronze Age and Iron Age pottery assemblages recovered from excavations in the county. The number of large scale excavations of sites of this period has shown that people tended to move around over time, often over a fairly limited area. As a result, the date span of any ceramic assemblage recovered can extend over a considerable period of time and space. In order to establish the date, size and possible population of Iron Age settlements it is therefore necessary to date pottery assemblages as closely as possible.

In addition to studying pottery from my own excavations, I have examined much of the material from other sites in the county. With the exception of the hillfort at Rainsborough and the ringwork at Thrapston, sites producing any amount of pottery dating to the first half of the millennium are relatively rare in the county. In contrast, sites dating to the second half of the millennium are more common and easier to locate. The pottery from two large excavations in the county – at Stanwick and Crick – has yet to be published and once this is done it will help create a type series for the region. In addition, there is an important group of pottery to be published from a site at Coton, near Rugby, just over the county border in Warwickshire.

The Criteria used for Classification

I have used five criteria to categorise and date the pottery assemblages. These are:

- colour, thickness, fabric, texture and surface finish;
- decoration;
- length of the neck;
- distinctive vessel forms, and;
- rim forms.

Different aspects of these critera are found in distinct phases of the late Bronze Age and Iron Age and can be used for closer dating of assemblages. Rim and neck forms can be particularly informative. Fabrics alone are rarely important as the majority of assemblages in all phases are predominantly shell-gritted. More detail on each criteria is shown below.

CATEGORY 1: Colour, Thickness, Fabric, Texture and Surface Finish

This category is often useful for assemblages consisting of body sherds with few if any diagnostic features. A number of characteristics can be considered:

- If the sherds are predominantly brown, buff or creamy-brown in colour they are unlikely to be any later in date than the early-middle Iron Age (EMIA). Thick-walled sherds that are black or red are most likely to date to the middle-late Iron Age (MLIA).

- An assemblage of thin-walled sherds is likely to date to the early part of the millennium. On some sites thin-walled sherds are found with an oxidized external surface and a black or grey inner surface (Oakley and Briar Hill) and are diagnostic of this late Bronze Age-early Iron Age phase (LB/EIA).

- Analysis has shown that the vast majority of pottery from Northamptonshire was made from locally available clay. Shelly fabrics occur widely in the county and they are of limited value in dating.

- On the whole, early Iron Age pottery tends to be better quality than that dating to later periods. The surface of the sherds can be burnished, smooth, course or harsh in most periods, but this may vary from site to site. Assemblages of sherds with course, harsh surfaces are most likely to date to the later periods.

CATEGORY 2: Decoration

Decoration can be an important diagnostic guide. The following styles are distinctive:

- Fingernail or finger tip decoration occurs in all phases in Northamptonshire. In the late Bronze Age-early Iron Age period impressions made with a finger or other tool are common on the outer edge of the rim (Briar Hill and Thrapston).

- Finger decoration is common on the shoulders of jars for a large part of the Iron Age, but is rarely found any later than the 4th century BC (Grendon and Brafield)

- Finger decoration on the top of the rim is not a good dating indicator, and varies from site to site. In Northamptonshire it seems to be most common in the middle Iron Age (Twywell).

- Surface decoration in zones or panels, as at Thrapston, dates mainly to the 8th–6th centuries BC.

- Decoration towards the end of the early Iron Age in Northamptonshire appears to consist of more lineal patterns, in the form of herringbone, zig-zags or swags, and also slash decoration, often on the neck.

- Curvilinear or La Tene decoration occurs mainly on globular or slack sided bowls and dates mainly to the middle-late Iron Age period (2nd and 1st centuries BC). This was unusually common at Weekley.

- Some of the scored ware at Weekley appears to be patterned, but much of this practice could be functional. This is found mainly on storage jars and dates principally from the 3rd century to the 1st century BC.

CATEGORY 3: Length of Neck

The length of the rim and neck is one of the most useful diagnostic characteristics. The majority of vessels dating to the early Iron Age and early-middle Iron Age (7th–4th centuries) have long rim or rim neck profiles. They get progressively shorter until the middle-late Iron Age when many vessels are virtually neckless.

In the late Bronze Age-early Iron Age period both types occur and caution is needed.

The length of the neck is determined by measuring the distance from the top of the rim to the centre of the neck. Varieties defined as having long necks (eg Gretton) have a minimum neck length of 12mm.

The following is a description of vessel types and their length of neck:

- A1 – vessels with long necks (up to and over 12mm);
- B1 – neckless vessels where the wall of the pot continues to a simple rim with no break in profile;
- B2 – vessels with short stubby rims, either upright, everted or expanded;
- B3 – jars with little or no neck and heavy expanded rims that are rolled over, rounded or oval;
- C1 – vessels with a concave neck.

Assemblages with the majority of types B2 and B3 are likely to date to the middle-late Iron Age (Weekley and Hunsbury). B1 types are found in all phases. C1 types are not easy to date but vessels with long profiles are probably the earlier.

CATEGORY 4: Distinctive Vessel Forms

The following vessel types can be diagnostic:

- Carinated bowls. These are most common in assemblages dating from the 7th–4th or early 3rd centuries, but have earlier origins. Bowls that have a broadly similar diameter at the rim and shoulder appear to be later in the sequence;
- Jars with a high, sharp or sharply-rounded shoulder, with or without decoration. These have a similar date range as carinated bowls.
- Globular bowls. This type of bowl is common in the middle-late Iron Age (Weekley and Hunsbury) but rare in the early middle Iron Age.

CATEGORY 5: Rim forms

- Rim tops. Rim tops are mostly round or flat. Both types occur throughout the millennium but flat-topped varieties are rare during the earlier phases.
- Plain rims that are not expanded either internally or externally are the most common form in all phases. If none of the neck survives the rims are generally poor dating indicators, but thin-walled rims are likely to be early.
- Expanded rim forms where they are in fashion for a limited amount of time, or have a functional use, can be good dating indicators, but many are probably shaped at the whim of the potter. Rims expanded internally are rare in the later periods.

The Proposed Ceramic Phases

The date range of the pottery from the sites I excavated in the late 1960s and 1970s spans most of the second half of the millennium and is therefore valuable in assessing the dates of other sites at this time. In addition, radiocarbon dates obtained from these sites – especially at Gretton, Twywell and Weekley – provide a good match with the proposed pottery typologies over this period.

Although radiocarbon dates can be unreliable for parts of the Iron Age period, the data from both Gretton and Twywell is more likely to be of this period. In addition, the 5th century Gretton date was supported by an iron ring headed pin of this period and the 3rd century date for Twywell was obtained by charred grain obtained *in situ*.

The dates from these sites are particularly important as this was a period when pottery styles appear to be changing. The pottery of the early and middle period was dominated by long-necked forms including high-necked jars, often with shoulder decoration and both carinated and round shouldered bowls. After this time, the necks of the vessels gradually get shorter and scored wares become increasingly common.

For example, at least 90% of the vessels from Gretton (5th century) were long necked, while over 90% of those from Weekley (3rd–1st century) were neckless or had short stubby rims. This also applies to the pottery from many other sites in the county that date to a period just before the introduction of late Iron Age Belgic types (i.e. 1st century BC).

The pottery from Twywell spans these two periods and styles. There are two pit groups at Twywell from different phases and the gradual change in neck length is illustrated in comparing the assemblages from the earlier and later group of pits.

Applying the criteria outlined above with radiocarbon dates produces a six-stage chronology as shown on the following page.

There are a number of other sites in the county without radiocarbon dates that have produced a substantial amount of pottery and could be assimilated within this chronology. These include:

- Brafield (5th–3rd century BC)
- Courtenhall (3rd century BC–1st century AD)
- Crick (4th–1st century BC, not published)
- Harringworth (3rd century BC)
- Hunsbury (2nd–1st century BC)
- Stanwick (not published)
- Wilby Way (5th–1st century BC)

PHASE	PERIOD	DATE	LOCATION AND TYPE OF SITE	RADIOCARBON DATES
1	Late Bronze Age/ Early Iron Age (LBA/EIA)	1000–650 BC	Thrapston, Ringwork	9th–7th century (2 dates).
			Great Oakley, 2 semi-circular structures, iron smelting and pits.	8th–6th century
2	Early Iron Age (EIA)	700–350 BC	Rainsborough, Hillfort	7th–5th century (4 dates)
			Gretton, pair of parallel ditches (Ditch A).	Mid 5th century (2 dates)
3	Early/Middle Iron Age (EMIA)	400–250 BC	Gretton, pair of parallel ditches (Ditch B)	Early 3rd century (2 dates)
			Brackmills, N'pton, pits, ditches and burial with torc.	Early 4th century
4	Middle Iron Age (MIA)	300–150 BC	Twywell, settlement site, charred grain *in situ* in pit.	3rd century
5	Middle/Late Iron Age (MLIA)	200 BC–20 AD	Weekley, settlement site, filling of recut ditch.	Late 3rd century – early 1st century AD (5 dates)
6	Late Iron Age (LIA)	50 BC–50 AD		No dates

A discussion of the individual phases follows.

PHASE 1: Late Bronze Age/Early Iron Age

There are four, mostly small, published assemblages of pottery of this period in the county. Pottery from sites further afield, particularly in the Thames Valley is useful for comparison (Barrett 1976 & Knight 1984).

Thrapston

The ringwork at Thrapston is the only site of this period to have produced a reasonable amount of pottery. Some of the pottery is decorated in the post Deverill Rimbury (PDR) decorated tradition. A feature of the assemblage is the number of rims decorated on the outer edge of the rim. Radiocarbon dates from the site suggest it dates from the 9th–7th centuries BC.

Oakley and Corby

Small assemblages of pottery of this period were found on two sites near Corby. The sherds, which were mostly small, came largely from a ditch at Corby and several pits at Oakley. The majority of the sherds derived from vessels with very thin walls and were mostly red-brown on the outer surface and grey-black internally. The sherds were all undecorated and may belong to the PDR plain ware phase. Two radiocarbon dates suggest a date of around the 8th century BC.

Brair Hill, Northampton

An assemblage of small weathered sherds was recovered from the pits of a pit alignment at Briar Hill. The sherds were probably residual in the filling of the pits. They were similar in appearance to those from Oakley and Corby, but a number were decorated in a style similar to material from Thrapston.

Upton, Northampton

Pottery of this period came from a pit alignment and several isolated pits.

Borough Hill, Daventry

Several late Bronze Age socketed axes were found on the hillfort suggesting occupation at that time. Excavation on the site revealed a number of features containing decorated pottery likely to date to this phase.

PHASE 2: Early Iron Age

There are two sites in the county which have produced good sized assemblages of pottery from this phase. Sites in neighbouroughing counties have produced pottery of this type including Fengate and West Harling in Cambridgeshire and Ivinghoe in Buckinghamshire.

Rainsborough

There are four radiocarbon dates, clustered around the 6th century. Although the site was clearly occupied over a long period of time much of the illustrated pottery probably dates to this period. The earliest pottery is notable for a number of tall slack-sided jars. There is a virtual absence of jars with a sharp (dog-leg) shoulder as well as carinated bowls, and the spare decoration is largely confined to the shoulder or neck.

Gretton (see Figure 1)

The ceramic assemblage from Gretton came from the fill of two parallel ditches. Two radiocarbon dates produced from charcoal found in Ditch A are centred on the middle of the 5th century BC and two dates from Ditch B were centred on the end of the 4th century BC suggesting an age difference of around 150 years between the pottery from the two ditches.

FACING PAGE
Figure 1 *Gretton*. Ditch A, layers 2 & 3. Early Iron Age (5th century BC). Illustrations by Pat Foster.

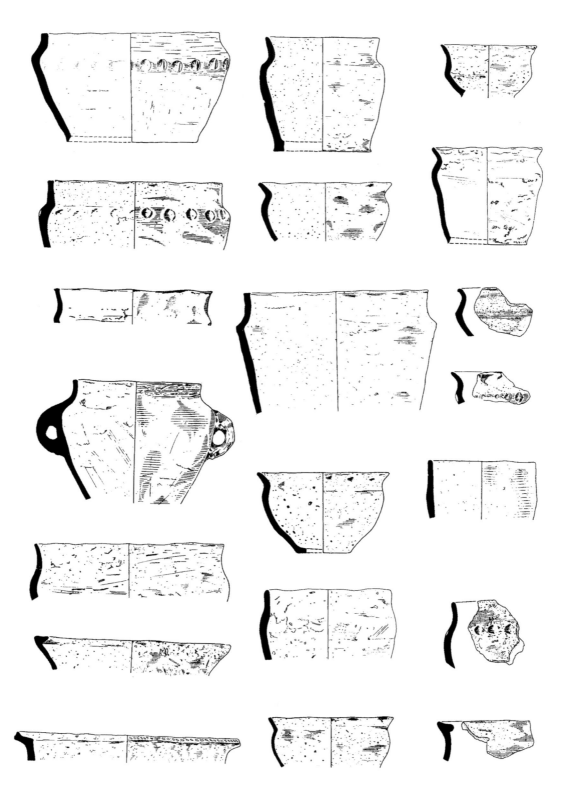

The pottery from Ditch A is relatively fresh and may have been dumped into the ditch over a short period of time, possibly during the 5th century. In contrast to the material from Rainsborough, the material contains many carinated and round shouldered bowls as well as sharp shouldered jars. Decoration is largely confined to finger impressions on the shoulders of jars. There is a limited number of jar forms with expanded rims and notable amongst these are vessels with a wide flange both internal and external. A related type sees the flanges folded back onto the neck of the vessels. Elsewhere, the assemblage is perhaps best compared with the pottery from sites to the east such as West Harling in Norfolk and Darmsden in Suffolk.

PHASE 2/3: Early/Middle Iron Age

There are a number of sites in the county where the ceramic assemblages may have their origins in Phase Two and then continue into Phase Three or later.

Brafield

Much of the pottery from this site came from one large pit, but there are no radiocarbon dates or stratigraphical relationships to assist with the dating. Professor Hawkes examined some of the pottery in 1962 and dated most of it to between 5th-3rd centuries BC.

The assemblage contains numerous sherds from carinated or round shouldered bowls, and the dates from Ditch B at Gretton suggest these vessels continue in use until the end of the 4th century at least. However, there is no scored ware from Brafield and it is perhaps unlikely that any of the pottery from the site dates to any later them the middle of the 3rd century.

The forms and decoration of the earliest pottery may suggest the assemblage originated earlier than Professor Hawkes suggested, but the devolved form of shouldered jars points to a middle Iron Age date for some of the material.

Wilby Way, Great Doddington

The pottery from the site at Wilby Way contains shouldered jars and carinated bowls that date to the early-middle Iron Age at the latest. Occupation on the site is then continuous until at least the end of the 2nd century BC. The decoration found on the early vessels together with the forms suggest the pottery may have been broadly contemporary with the material from Brafield.

PHASE 3: Early/Middle Iron Age

In many respects the pottery from this phase and that from the previous phase is similar and it is difficult to define when this phase begins. The end of this period is marked by the phasing out of carinated bowls and sharp shouldered bowls, both plain and decorated, and by the introduction of vessels with shorter necks and also scored wares. The radiocarbon dates from Gretton (below) suggest this phase ends sometime in the 3rd century BC.

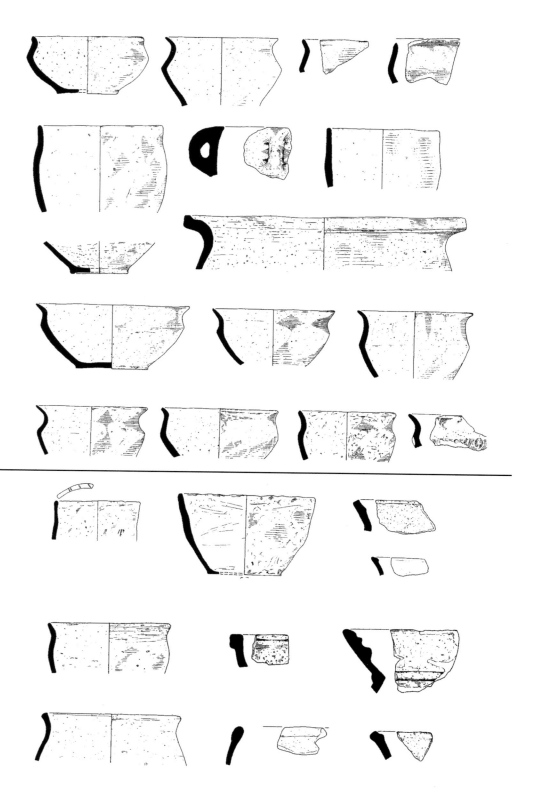

Gretton, Ditch B (see Figure 2)

Dates in the early 3rd century came from charcoal found in the lower layers of Ditch B at Gretton. The pottery from this layer still contains carinated bowls and stylistically there is little difference to that in Ditch A. However, changes appear in the upper layers of the ditch where vessels with a distinctive square headed rim were found along with a vessel with a long evened neck which was grooved or corrugated internally. The pottery is still of good quality with none of the coarse scored wares common in the area in the later periods.

Harringworth

An assemblage of pottery came from a pair of parallel ditches situated a mile to the north of the site at Gretton. The assemblage contains no obvious carinated forms, but it includes variations of the square-headed rim found at Gretton. A feature of the pottery found in the ditches is the number of thickened or expanded rim forms. Scored wares were found in later features on the site but did not occur in the assemblage from the parallel ditches. This pottery may be transitional between phases three and four.

Other sites

The earliest pottery from the sites at Courtenhall and Twywell (below) date to this phase but the majority belongs to later phases. This is a similar pattern in a number of other sites in the county, including Brackmills, Northampton, with an early 4th century date from an early pit. Just outside the county there are important assemblages at Milton Keynes and Coton Park, Rugby.

Sherds from decorated vessels that date to this phase or earlier have been found on a number of sites in the county. These include examples with swag decoration from Crick, Northampton (Pensvale) and Raunds, and others with chevron or wavy-line decoration from sites at Brigstock, Islip and Wellingborough. Decoration on the rim is rare during this phase.

PHASE 4: Middle Iron Age

Sites that have produced assemblages of pottery dating to this phase (and the later Phase Five) are very common in Northamptonshire, but in many cases the assemblage is small or unpublished. The pottery from Twywell represents the best collection of middle Iron Age pottery in the county.

Twywell (see Figure 3)

A quantity of the earlier pottery found on this site was recovered from a number of pits alongside charred grain which was carbon dated to around the beginning of the 3rd century BC. At the other end of the date range, a single sherd of curvilinear decorated pottery came from one of the pits which would extend into the later phase.

FACING PAGE
Figure 3 *Twywell*.
TOP GROUP: Earliest phase, middle Iron Age (3rd–2nd century BC).
BOTTOM GROUP: Second phase, middle Iron Age (3rd–2nd century BC).
Illustrations by Marian Cox.

OVERLEAF, LEFT PAGE
Figure 4 *Weekley*.
Middle/Late Iron Age (3rd century BC-20AD).
Illustrations by Pat Foster.

OVERLEAF, RIGHT PAGE
Figure 5 *Weekley*.
Late 1st century BC–mid 1st century AD (50BC–50AD).
Illustrations by Pat Foster.

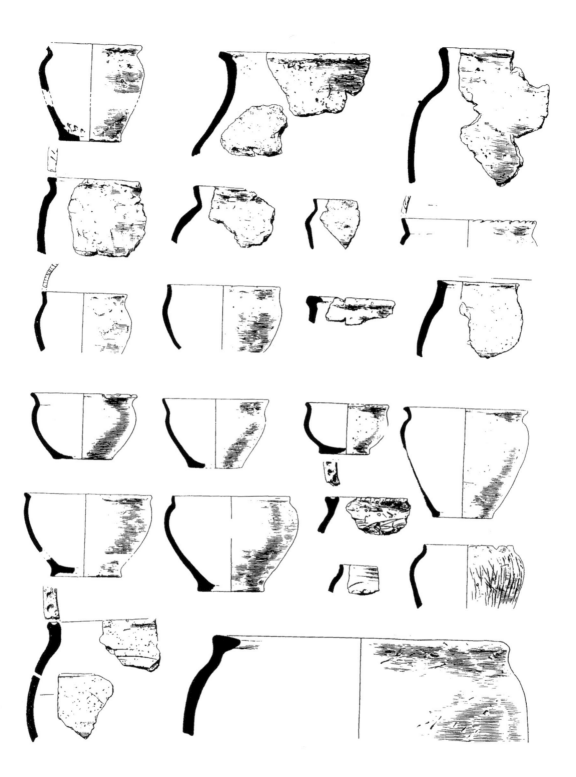

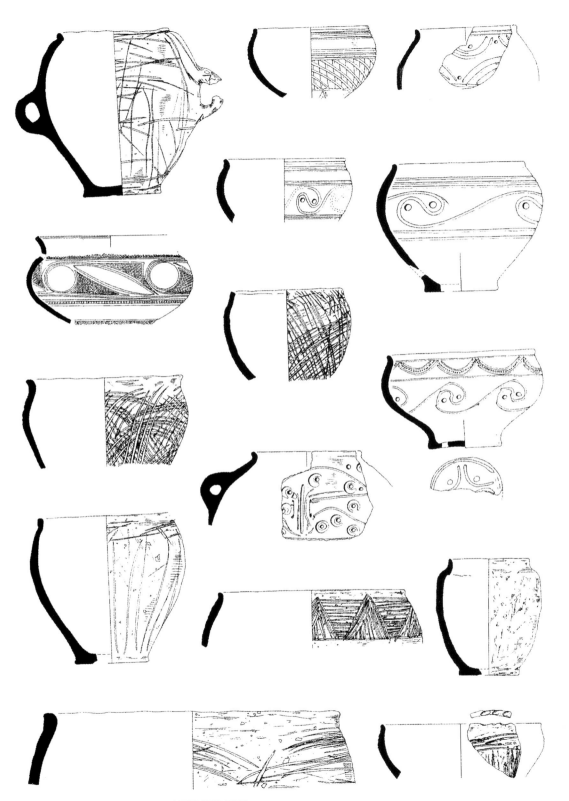

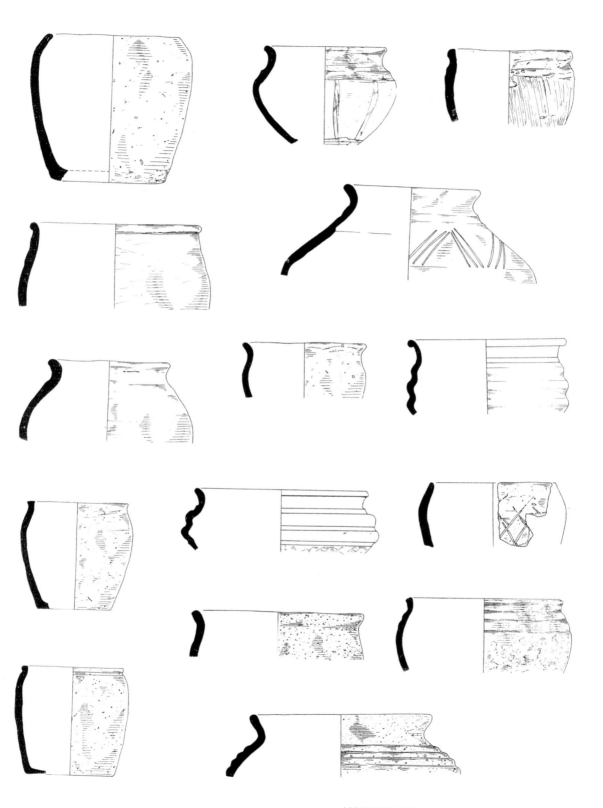

The pottery from this phase includes a quantity of scored wares and in general the vessels have shorter necks than those in the earlier period. Jars with expanded or thickened rims become common and many rims are decorated with finger nail or thumb impressions on the top. Bowls tend to be round shouldered and of ovid form.

Other sites

Pottery from this phase is included in assemblages from Wilby Way, Doddington, Courtenhall and Brackmills, Northampton. On both sites there are jars with expanded rims but decorated rims and scored wares are less common. Unpublished assemblages include those from Crick, Stanwick and Wollaston.

PHASE 5: Middle/Late Iron Age

It is uncertain when this phase originated – and it may have been gradual or occurred at different times in different parts of the county – but it is presumed it began sometime after the late 3rd century and continued into the 1st century AD. Pottery from this period has been found on many sites in the county with Weekley and Hunsbury representing the type sites for this phase.

Weekley (see Figure 4)

The site at Weekley was notable for the large amount of decorated pottery recovered. Vessels dating to this phase often have little if any neck and tend to be globular or slack-sided in profile. The rims of the bowls are usually direct or slightly upturned, wheras the jars often have heavy expanded rims, the expansion being external and either rounded, oval or rectangular in form.

There are five radiocarbon dates from a ditch at Weekley, ranging in date from the late 3rd century to the early 1st century AD, (with a recommended central date of around 75BC). The five charcoal samples used for dating all came from a layer that produced a lot of decorated pottery of La Tene type.

Hunsbury

Although there is an earlier phase of pottery from Hunsbury, the majority is later and similar to the material from Weekley. The main difference between the two assemblages is in the number of large jars at Hunsbury. Some of the Hunsbury vessels have slightly longer necks, perhaps suggesting that this phase originated earlier here than at Weekley.

Phase 6: Late Iron Age

Pottery from this phase occurs on many sites in the county but there are particularly well stratified groups from Aldwincle and Weekley (see Figure 5 and above). Other sites where pottery has been found include Rushden and a number of sites around Northampton, including Courtenhall, Duston, Brackmills, Moulton Park and Hardingstone.

Radiocarbon Dates by Andy Chapman

Table of radiocarbon dates for sites excavated by Dennis Jackson

Site	Feature/Phase (sample)	Radiocarbon Age BP (Lab No)	Calibrated date (Cal BC) 68% confidence 95% confidence
Great Oakley (Jackson 1982, 5-6)	Area 1, pit F9 (charcoal)	2630+/-90 (Har4994)	910-540 (910-750, 50%) **1000-400**
	Area 2 pits F28-29 (charcoal)	2500+/-80 (Har4064)	790-510 **800-400**
Hunsbury Hill (Jackson 1994, 18)	layer 9 behind rear revetment (charred plank)	2420+/-100 (Har 10569)	760-390 (560-390, 40%) **800-200**
	Rampart (charred post)	2390+/-70 (Har10568)	760-390 (550-390, 50%) **800-350**
	Rear revetment (charred post)	2310+/-70 (Har10570)	490-200 (420-200, 63%) **800-150**
Gretton (Jackson 1985, 81, table 1)	Ditch A (charcoal mature wood)	2410+/-80 (Har-3015)	760-390 (550-390, 44%) **790-370**
	Ditch A (charcoal mature wood)	2390+/-60 (Har-2760)	760-390 (540-390, 53%) **770-380**
	Ditch B (charcoal mature wood)	2240+/-70 (Har-3014)	390-200 **410-90**
	Ditch B (charcoal mature wood)	2210+/-70 (Har-2761)	380-190 **400-90**
Twywell (Jackson 1975, 33-34 & 73)	Pit 132 Early Phase (charred grain)	2230+/-90 (NPL-225)	400-180 **550-0**
Weekley (Jackson 1985-87, 49)	Ditch K1 (charcoal)	2160+/-70 (Har-1725)	360-90 (260-90, 45%) **390-40**
	Ditch K1 (charcoal)	2120+/-90 (Har-1725)	360-40 (240-40, 54%) **390 Cal BG-60 CalAD**
	Ditch K1 (charcoal)	2050+/-70 (Har-1725)	170 Cal BG-30 Cal AD **350 Cal BG-130 CalAD** (210-90 CalAD, 91%)
	Ditch K1 (charcoal)	2000+/-70 (Har-1725)	100 Cal BG-90 CalAD **200 CalBC-140 CalAD**
	Ditch K1 (charcoal)	1910+/-80 (Har-1725)	0-220 CalAD **100 Cal BG-330 CalAD**

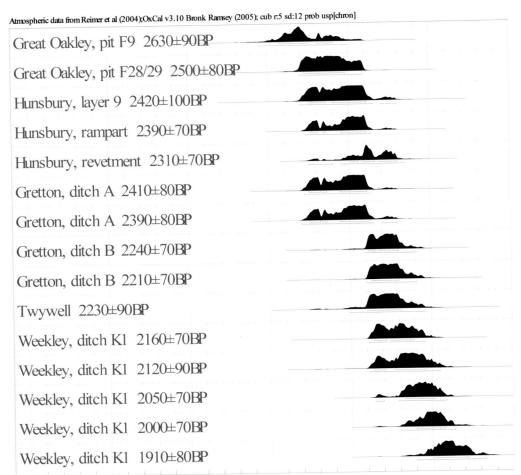

Atmospheric data from Reimer et al (2004);OxCal v3.10 Bronk Ramsey (2005); cub r:5 sd:12 prob usp[chron]

Great Oakley, pit F9 2630±90BP

Great Oakley, pit F28/29 2500±80BP

Hunsbury, layer 9 2420±100BP

Hunsbury, rampart 2390±70BP

Hunsbury, revetment 2310±70BP

Gretton, ditch A 2410±80BP

Gretton, ditch A 2390±80BP

Gretton, ditch B 2240±70BP

Gretton, ditch B 2210±70BP

Twywell 2230±90BP

Weekley, ditch K1 2160±70BP

Weekley, ditch K1 2120±90BP

Weekley, ditch K1 2050±70BP

Weekley, ditch K1 2000±70BP

Weekley, ditch K1 1910±80BP

2500CalBC   2000CalBC   1500CalBC   1000CalBC   500CalBC   CalBC/CalAD   500CalAD

Calibrated date

List of other quoted radiocarbon dates

Thrapston ringwork (Hull 2000-1): 840-785 Cal BC, 68% confidence;
910-760 Cal BC, 95% confidence; 2630+/- 50 BP; BM-3113 and 810-600 Cal BC,
68% confidence; 810-540 Cal BC, 98% confidence; 2540+/-35 BP; BM-3129.

Rainsborough hillfort (Avery 1967) (earliest and latest of four with low errors):
770-540 Cal BC, 68% confidence; 780-410, 95% confidence; 2490 +/-35 BP;
UB-737 and 750-400 Cal BC, 68% confidence; 770-390 Cal BC, 98% confidence;
2430 +/- 75 BP; UB-853.

Brackmills (Great Houghton), Northampton (Chapman 2000-1): intercept,
390 Cal BC; 405-370 Cal BC, 68% confidence; 505-205 Cal BC, 95% confidence;
2320+/-60 BP, Beta-116571.

Note: All calibrated dates generated from OxCal v3.10

Excavations and Watching Briefs Carried Out by Dennis Jackson

PARISH (Site)		NGR	NE	BA	IA	R	AS	ME	SITE TYPE	WORK*	Report	Notes
ALDWINCLE	(Gravel quarry)	SP993803	■	■					Monumental burials	EX/1968-9	9	
		SP999801				■			Bridge	EX1968-9	8	
		SP992800			■				Enclosure/Ditches	EX/1971	11	
		SP999805	■	■					Monuments/PA	EX/1971	9	
		SP999805					■		Water hole/Burials	LX/1971	11	
AYNO	(M40 motorway)	SP513318	■						Pits	WB-LE/1990		12
		SP505318				■			Ditches	WB-LE/1990		12
BRIGSTOCK		SP925841		■	■				Settlement	EX/1979-81	19	
	(Bypass)	SP931852				■	■		Ditches	WB/1985		10
BRIXWORTH		SP961699				■			Settlement	EV/1990		11
BULWICK		SP9294				■			Iron working	EX/1969	14	
	(Fina pipeline)	SP965950			■				Settlement	WB/1990	28	
BYFIELD		SP505515				■			Iron working	LX/1985	23	
CHAPEL BRAMPTON		SP731646			■	■			Kiln/SSB	EV/1990		11
CORBY	(Stockholme Close)	SP863896		■	■				Ditches/PA	EV/1974	18	
	(Viking Way)	SP856868			■				Enclosure	EX/1974	18	
DAVENTRY	(Borough Hill)	SP380620		■	■				Hillfort	EV/1983/91	34	
DEENETHORPE	(Fina pipeline)	SP971912			■	■			Settlement	WB/1990	28	
DENFORD		SP922682			■				Ditches	LE/1990	28	
DITCHFORD		SP923682			■				Ditches	WB/1980s		11
EARLS BARTON		SP870627		■					Barrow	EX/1968	2 & 20	
ECTON		SP823651		■					Cremations	LE/1969	3	
FINESHADE	(Fina pipeline)	SP968976				■			Kiln/Barn	LE/1990	28	
GEDDINGTON		SP875826			■				Roundhouse	EX/1977	15	
GREAT HARROWDEN		SP830707			■				Ditches	WB		11
GREAT OAKLEY		SP881866		■	■				Settlement	EX/1976-78	18	
GRENDON		SP870880		■					Barrows/PA	WB-LE/1975-9	35	
		SP881615				■			Vineyard	EX/1975	35	
GRETTON		SP910946			■				PA/Currency	EX/1978-9	5	
		SP908944		■	■				Ditches/Post holes	EX/1978-9	21	
		SP909945				■			Iron working	EX/1969	14	

PARISH (Site)		NGR	PERIOD						SITE TYPE	WORK*	PUB.**	
			NE	BA	IA	R	AS	ME			Report	Notes
HARRINGWORTH		SP930970	■	■					Pits	LX/1970/7	13	
		SP930968			■				Ditches/Pits	LX/1978	17	
		SP936981				■			Building	EX/1972	17	
		SP924960				■			Iron working	WB-LX/1972-3	Unpublished.	
		SP941470					■		Enclosure	EV/1979	17	
HEMMINGTON		TL095852						■	Building	WB/1985		10
ISLIP		SP983786			■				Ditches	LX/1981		6
LAXTON		SP068971				■			Iron working	EX/1985	23	
LITTLE HOUGHTON		SP8059	■						Pit/Ditches	WB-LE/1978		3
KINGS SUTTON	(M40 Motorway)	SP499345			■				Pits	WB-LE/1990		12
NORTHAMPTON	(Briar Hill)	SP740589	■	■					PA	EX/1969	5	
	(Grange Wood)	SP741575		■	■				Pit/Ditches	WB/1979		11
	(Hunsbury)	SP735583			■				Hillfort	EX/1988	30	
	(Hunsbury environs)	SP7358		■	■		■		Pits/Ditches	WB-LX/1985-90	31	
	(Pensvale)	SP751577		■					Pits	WB-LX/1990		15
	(Wootton Hill Farm)	SP738578			■				Enclosure	EX/1986	24	
NORTON	(M40 Motorway)	SP612643				■			Ditches	WB/1986		10
OUNDLE		TL033880				■			SSB	EX/1979		4
		TL025893			■				Enclosure	WB/1977		2
RAUNDS	(Fina pipeline)	TL009727			■				Settlement	WB/1990	28	
RINGSTEAD		SP977748				■			Building	EX/1971	16	
		SP9775	■						Various	WB-LX/1970s		1
ROTHERSTHORPE		SP714575						■	Ditches	WB/1980		7
RUSHTON		SP850837			■				Ditches	EX/1970	10	
STANION		SP910866			■				Ditches	WB/1977		2
		SP926860				■			Pits	LE/1978		3
STANWICK		SP971710				■			Building/Ditches	EV/1979		4
		SP968712				■			Ditches	WB-LX/1984		9
SULGRAVE		SP557454						■	Post holes	LX/1980		7
THRAPSTON	(Chancery Lane)	SP996788					■		Mound/Burials	WB/1969		1
	(Huntingdon Road)	TL002787		■					Ringwork	EV/1991		14
TOWCESTER	(Cinema)	SP693485				■			Defences	WB/1982		8
	(158 Watling street)	SP691489				■			Defences	EV/1990		13
TWYWELL		SP952787			■	■			Settlement	EX/1966-7	7	
UPTON		SP713602			■		■		Ditches/SSB	EX/1965	1	
		Parish						■	Field Survey	S/1991	32	
WAKERLEY		SP995994					■		Cemetery	EX/1969-71	25	
		SP941983		■	■				Settlement	EX/1972-5	12	
WARMINGTON		TL053924		■					Barrow	EV/1979		5
WEEKLEY		SP886881			■				Settlement	EX/1975-78	22	
		SP886881				■			Lime kiln	EX/1971	6	
	(Weekley Hall Wood)	SP874813			■				Settlement	EX/1969	10	

PARISH (Site)	NGR	PERIOD						SITE TYPE	WORK*	PUB.**	
		NE	BA	IA	R	AS	ME			Report	Notes
WELDON	SP922886		▓					Burials		4	
WELLINGBOROUGH (Stanwell)	SP870690			▓				Settlement	EX/1986		
WOLLASTON	SP902625			▓	▓			PA/Buillding/SSB	EX/1984	29	
YARDLEY GOBION	SP770446			▓				Pit/Ditch	WB/		11
YARDLEY HASTINGS	SP876571					▓	▓	Ditches/Buildings	EX/1982	33	

* WORK - Type of work carried out and year:

      EX - Excavation

      LX - Limited excavation

      EV - Evaluation

      WB - Watching brief

      S - Survey

** PUBLICATION REFERENCE

      See Appendix 4 for published reports and Notes

Publications by Dennis Jackson

Reports

1. 1969. The Iron Age and Anglo-Saxon Site at Upton, Northants. *Antiq J.,* XlIX, 202–221.

2. 1972. The Earls Barton Barrow. *Current Archaeology*, 32, 328–341.

3. 1973. Excavations at North Lodge, Ecton, Northamptonshire. *Northamptonshire Archaeology*, 8, 31–38.

4. 1974. Bronze Age Burials at Weldon. *Northamptonshire Archaeology*, 9, 3–12.

5. 1974. Two New Pit Alignments and a Hoard of Currency Bars from Northamptonshire. *Northamptonshire Archaeology*, 9, 13–45.

6. 1975. A Roman Lime Kiln at Weekley, Northants. *Brittania*, IV, 128–140.

7. 1975. An Iron Age Site at Twywell, Northamptonshire. *Northamptonshire Archaeology*, 10, 31–39.

8. 1976. A Roman Timber Bridge at Aldwincle, Northants. *Britannia*, VII, 39–72.

9. 1976. The Excavation of Neolithic and Bronze Age Sites at Aldwincle, Northants. *Northamptonshire Archaeology*, 11, 12–70.

10. 1976. Two Iron Age Sites North of Kettering, Northants. *Northamptonshire Archaeology*, 11, 71–86.

11. 1977. Further Excavations at Aldwincle, Northamptonshire. *Northamptonshire Archaeology*, 12, 9–54.

12. 1978. Excavations at Wakerley, Northants, 1972–75. *Britannia*, IX, 115–242.

13. 1978. Neolithic and Bronze Age Activity in the Harringworth Area. *Northamptonshire Archaeology*, 13, 3–8.

14. 1979. Roman Ironworking at Bulwick and Gretton. *Northamptonshire Archaeology*, 14, 31–37

15. 1979. A Middle Iron Age Site at Gedddington. *Northamptonshire Archaeology*, 15, 12–34.

16. 1980. Roman Buildings at Ringstead, Northants. *Northamptonshire Archaeology*, 15, 12–23.

17. 1981. Archaeology in an Ironstone Quarry in the Harringworth-Wakerley Area, 1968–79. *Northamptonshire Archaeology*, 16, 7–32.

18. 1982. Great Oakley and Early Iron Age Sites in the Corby Area. *Northamptonshire Archaeology*, 17, 3–23.

19. 1983. The Excavation of an Iron Age Site at Brigstock, Northants, 1979–81. *Northamptonshire Archaeology*, 18, 7–32.

20. 1984. The Excavation of a Bronze Age Barrow at Earls Barton, Northants. *Northamptonshire Archaeology*, 19, 3–30.

21. 1985. An Early Iron Age and Beaker Site at Gretton, Northants, 1979–81. *Northamptonshire Archaeology*, 20, 67–86 (with D. Knight).

22. 1986–7. Late Iron Age and Roman Settlement at Weekley in Northants. *Northamptonshire Archaeology*, 21, 41–94.

23. 1988. Two New Romano–British Ironworking Sites in Northamptonshire – A New Type of Furnace. *Brittania*, XIX, 275–298 (with R Tylecote).

24. 1988–89. An Iron Age Enclosure at Wootton Hill Farm, Northampton. *Northamptonshire Archaeology*, 23, 3–21.

25. 1988–89. The Anglo–Saxon Cemetery at Wakerley, Northamptonshire, Excavations by Mr D Jackson, 1968–69. *Northamptonshire Archaeology*, 23, 69–183 (report mainly by B. Adams and L. Badenoch).

26. 1989. Some Late Iron Age Defended Enclosures in Northamptonshire. *Midlands Prehistory*, BAR British Series 204, 158–179 (with B. Dix).

27. 1991. Archaeological Evaluations at Wollaston. *Northamptonshire Archaeology*, 23, 82–85.

28. 1991. The FINA Pipeline Project and a Roman Pottery Kiln at Fineshade, *Northamptonshire Archaeology*, 23, 85–92.

29. 1992. Wollaston Bypass, Northamptonshire. Salvage Excavations 1984. *Northamptonshire Archaeology*, 24, 67–76 (with A. Chapman).

30. 1993–94. Excavations of the Hillfort Defences at Hunsbury, Northampton in 1952 and 1988. *Northamptonshire Archaeology*, 25, 5–20.

31. 1993–94. Iron Age and Anglo-Saxon Settlement and Activity Around the Hunsbury Hillfort, Northampton. *Northamptonshire Archaeology*, 25, 69–78.

32. 1993–94. Archaeological Evaluation at Upton, Northampton. *Northamptonshire Archaeology*, 25, 69–78.

33. 1993–94. Anglo-Saxon Occupation at Yardley Hastings, Northants. *Northamptonshire Archaeology*, 25, 93–98 (with G. Foard).

34. 1993–94. The Iron Age Hillfort at Borough Hill, Daventry: Excavations in 1983. *Northamptonshire Archaeology*, 25, 63–68.

35. 1995. Excavations at Grendon Gravel Quarry: Part 2: Other rehistoric, Iron Age and later sites excavated in 1974–75 and further observations between 1976–80. *Northamptonshire Archaeology*, 26, 3–32.

36. 1996–97. Further Excavations at Borough Hill, Daventry, Northants. *Northamptonshire Archaeology*, 27, 143–146.

37. 1998–99. Titchmarsh Late Iron Age and Roman Settlement, *Northamptonshire Archaeology*, 28 (with M. Cuteis and P. Markham).

Notes in Archaeological Reports

1. 1977. Northamptonshire Archaeology, 12, 190–191
2. 1978. Northamptonshire Archaeology, 13, 103–104
3. 1979. Northamptonshire Archaeology, 14, 102–104
4. 1980. Northamptonshire Archaeology, 15, 168–170
5. 1981. Northamptonshire Archaeology, 16, 200
6. 1982. Northamptonshire Archaeology, 17, 91–93
7. 1982. Northamptonshire Archaeology, 17, 102–103
8. 1983-4. Northamptonshire Archaeology, 19, 152
9. 1985. Northamptonshire Archaeology, 20, 148
10. 1986-7. Northamptonshire Archaeology, 21, 154–157
11. 1991. Northamptonshire Archaeology, 23, 107–112
12. 1991. Northamptonshire Archaeology, 23, 118
13. 1992. Northamptonshire Archaeology, 24, 24–25
14. 1992. Northamptonshire Archaeology, 24, 95–96
15. 1993-4. Northamptonshire Archaeology, 25, 440–441

Notes

1   The Western Claylands. The description of the area used by Cambridgeshire County Council in their Landscape Character Assessment of the county. www.cambidgeshire.gov.uk/environment/countryside/ natureconservation/policy/guidelines.htm.

2   Lutton lies a mile and a half to the south-west of Washingly and has in the past been known as Lutton-cum-Washingley. In his excellent and comprehensive history of the village, titled Mucky Lutton, the author, Bert Saville, attributes the name to the 'nasty, sticky boulder clay' that dominates the area.

3   The population in 1801 was 95; it declined to 88 in 1851 and 61 by 1901. From 1931 Washingley was incorporated in the parish of Folksworth.

4   The Manor was equally divided between Eustace the Sheriff and Chetelbert the king's thegn or lord. The land passed into the possession of Walter de Washingley in 1166 and remained within this family for almost three centuries. His son, Richard de Washingley, was lord in 1201 when his brother John de Washingly accused him of killing his father. Richard was subsequently acquitted and the sherriff was ordered to arrest John and put him in prison.

5   The Manor passed from the de Washingleys to the Otter family and then to the Apreece family when Joan Otter, daughter and heiress of John Otter married Robert Apreece. The Apreeces came from an ancient family of Welsh nobles, descending from Blethin ap Maenarch, Prince of Brecknock. They were a staunchly catholic family; Robert Apreece, born in 1545, was referred to by the Bishop of Peterborough as 'that notorious recusant'. His grandson and heir, Robert, was murdered after the taking of Lincoln by the Parliamentary soldiers who shot him in cold blood on affirmation that he was 'Apreece the Roman Catholic'. Thomas Hussey Apreece, Captain of the Huntingdonshire Militia, held the manor in the late eighteenth century and was created a baronet in 1782 for his defence of Alnwick against the pirate Paul Jones. His surviving son, Sir George Thomas Apreece, died unmarried in 1842, and all the Washington property was given to St. Georges Hospital, London as no single relative was mentioned in his will.

6   It is known that Charles Bridgeman, the early eighteenth century
     naturalistic garden designer and Royal Gardener for Queen Anne, bought
     an inn for his wife in Stilton and he may have been involved in the
     design of the garden at the Hall.

7   Taylor, C., 1979. Roads and Tracks of Britain. London: Dent.

8   Any person who could read and write could open a 'Dame School' in
     their house without needing any teaching qualifications. Their living was
     made from the penny received each week from children attending the
     school. It is thought that Mary Cheney, described as a schoolmistress on
     her marriage certificate in 1844 ran such a school from School Cottage in
     Lutton, a practice that was continued by her daughter Ann Cheney until
     the opening of the village school in 1876 (Saville, 1992, pg 100).

9   Estimated by Saville (1992, pg 90).

10   A number of local graziers are recorded as Washingley residents in the
     burial records in Lutton Church, e.g. William Earl, grazier of Washingley
     died 1728, Thomas Richardson, grazier of Washingley died 1729.

11   Bate, J., 2003. John Clare A Biography. London: Picador, page 65.

12   Sinclair, I., 2005. Edge of the Orison. London:Hamish Hamilton.

13   Johnson, A.G, Bellamy, B & Foster, P.J. 1996, Excavations at Southwick,
     Northamptonshire, Northamptonshire Archaeology Vol 29 (2000-2001).

14   The passage of blood in the urine often caused by exposure to severe
     temperatures

15   Figures on the number of casualties during the First World War vary
     according to different sources, but it is generally accepted that around
     5.9m servicemen from the UK were mobilised, of which around
     660,00 were killed, 2m wounded and 340,000 missing (source: www.
     firstworldwar.com).

16   In Thomas Hardy's, Tess of the d'Urbervilles, the heroine's peasant father,
     Jack Durbeyfield, is mistakenly informed by an amateur genealogist that
     he is descended from a noble Norman family, the d'Urbervilles, with
     tragic consequences for himself and Tess.

17 John Dryden (1631-1700) was born in the rectory of All Saints Aldwincle. He was an influential poet, literary critic and playwright who dominated the literary life of Restoration England to the extent that the period became known as the 'Age of Dryden'.

18 Thomas Fuller (1608-1661) was born in the rectory of St Peter's in Aldwincle. He was a churchman and historian known for his writings, especially the 'Worthies of England' published after his death.

19 400-180 Cal BC, 68% confidence, 2230+/- 90BP, NPL-225.

20 3520-3020 Cal BC, 98% confidence, 4560 +/- 70BP, Har-141.

21 AD 137-180

22 680-990 Cal AD, 95% confidence, 1180+/-70 BP, Har-1185.

23 1630-1310 Cal BC, 95% confidence, 3210+/- 60BP, BM-681: 1530-1310 Cal BC, 95% confidence, 3170+/-50BP, BM-680.

24 The Royal Commission on Historical Monuments, 1960. A Matter of Time, an archaeological survey of the river gravels of England. London: HM Stationery Office.

25 Planning Policy Guidance 16: Archaeology and Planning was introduced by the British Government in 1990. This guidance outlines the importance of archaeology within the planning process, either through the preservation of remains in situ or by recording prior to their destruction by development. As part of this process, potential developers are now required to carry out (or commission) an archaeological evaluation of an area (at their expense) to be submitted to the local planning authority as part of the devlopment process.

26 Pearson, G (1979) Hooligan: A History of Respectable Fears.

27 The National Mapping Programme (NMP) carried out by English Heritage is an attempt to analyse the extensive collection of material held within the aerial photograph archives. Northamptonshire was one of the first counties to be included in the programme and the results were published in 'Mapping Ancient Landscapes in Northamptonshire' (2008), edited by Glen Foard and Alison Deegan.

Select Bibliography

Avery, M. 1967: Rainsborough, Northamptonshire, England: Excavations 1961-1965. *Proceedings of the Prehistoric Society* Vol 33, 202-306.

Barrett, J. 1976: *Deverel-Rimbury: Problems of Chronology and Interpretation,* in Burgess , C (ed) *Settlement and Economy in the Third and Second Millenia BC,* 289-307. Oxford.

Brewster, T.C.M. 1963: *The Excavation of Staple Howe.*

Chapman, A. 2000-01: Excavation of an Iron Age Settlement and Middle Saxon Cemetery at Great Houghton, Northampton, *Northamptonshire Archaeology,* Vol 29, 1-41

Chapman, A. 2007: A Bronze Age Barrow Cemetery and Later Boundaries, Pit Alignments and Enclosures at Gayhurst Quarries, Newport Pagnell. *Records of Buckinghamshire,* Vol 47 part 2, 83-211.

Clark, J.G.D. and Fell, C.I. 1953: An Early Iron Site at Micklmoor Hill, West Harling, Norfolk and its Pottery. *Proceedings of the Prehistoric Society,* Vol 19, 1-40.

Cotton, M.A. and Frere, S.S. 1968: Irvinghoe Beacon: Excavations 1963-65. *Records of Buckinghamshire,* 187-260.

Cunliffe, B. 1968: Early pre-Roman Communities in Eastern England. *Antiquaries Journal,* Vol 48, 175-191.

Cunliffe, B. 1978:*Iron Age Communities in England.* London.

Fell, C.I. 1937: The Hunsbury Hillfort, Northants, A new Survey of the Material. *Antiquaries Journal,* Vol 93, 57-100.

Foard, G. and Deegan, A. (eds). 2008: *Mapping Ancient Landscapes in Northamptonshire.* English Heritage.

Forde-Johnstone, J. 1966: *Hillforts of the Iron Age in England and Wales.* Liverpool.

Gibson, A. (ed) 1989: *Midland Prehistory. Some Recent and Current Researches into the Prehistory of Central England.* BAR British Series 204.

Grimes, W.F. 1961: *Draughton, Coldersworth and Heathrow,* in Frere, S.S. *Problems of the Iron Age in Southern Britain,* 21-8. London.

Hull, G. 2000-1: A Late Bronze Age Ringwork, Pits and Later Features at Thrapston, Northamptonshire. *Northamtonshire Archaeology,* Vol 29, 73-92.

Jones, L. Woodward, A. and Butuex, S. 2006: *Iron Age, Roman and Saxon Occupation at Grange Park. Excavations at Courteenhall, Northamptonshire 1999.* BAR British Series 425.

Knight, D. 1984: *Late Bronze Age and Iron Age Settlement in the Nene and Great Ouse Basins*. BAR British Series 130.

Last, J. 2005: Life by the River: A Prehistoric Landscape at Grendon, Northamptonshire. *Proceedings of the Prehistoric Society,* Vol 71, 333-360.

Pollard, J. 1996: Iron Age Riverside Pit Alignments at St Ives, Cambridgeshire. *Proceedings of the Prehistoric Society,* Vol 62, 93-115

Prior, F. 1984: *Excavations at Fengate, Peterborough; the 4th Report.* Northamptonshire Archaeological Society Monograph 2. Northampton.

Saville, B. 1992: *Mucky Lutton, the Yesterdays of a Northamptonshire Village.* Lutton Parochial Church Council.

Smith, C.A. 1975: *Excavations at Fisherwick, Staffordshire.* University of Nottingham.

Williams, J.H. 1974: *Two Iron Age Sites in Northamptonshire.* Northampton Development Corporation.

Williams, R.J. 1974: *Bancroft: the Late Bronze Age and Iron Age Settlements and Roman Temple Mausoleum.* Buckinghamshire Archaeological Society Monograph 7. Milton Keynes.

Woods, P.J. 1969: *Excavations at Hardingstone, Northants, 1967-8.* Northamptonshire County Council.

Index of Local Place Names